Anonymous

An treas leabhar Gaedhilge:

Third Irish book

Anonymous

An treas leabhar Gaedhilge:
Third Irish book

ISBN/EAN: 9783337723880

Printed in Europe, USA, Canada, Australia, Japan

Cover: Foto ©ninafisch / pixelio.de

More available books at **www.hansebooks.com**

AN TREAS LEABAR GAEDILGE.

THIRD IRISH BOOK.

PUBLISHED FOR THE

Society for the Preservation of the Irish Language.

Sixth Edition.
Tenth and Eleventh Thousand,

DUBLIN
M. H. GILL & SON.
1889.
[*All Rights Reserved.*]

SOCIETY
FOR THE
Preservation of the Irish Language.

OFFICERS AND COUNCIL ELECTED, ST. PATRICK'S DAY, 1889, FOR YEAR, 1889-90.

Patron.
(*Permanent*).
HIS GRACE THE MOST REV. T. W. CROKE, D.D.
Archbishop of Cashel.

President.
RIGHT HON. THE O'CONOR DON, P.C., D.L., M.R.I.A.

Vice-Presidents.
REV. SAMUEL HAUGHTON, M.D., D.C.L., F.R.S., S.F.T.C.D., President, Royal Irish Academy.
THE MOST REV. JOHN MACCARTHY, D.D., Bishop of Cloyne.
MARSHAL MACMAHON, Ex-Pres. of the French Republic.
THE MOST REV. PIERSE POWER, D.D., Bishop of Waterford and Lismore.

Hon. Treasurers.
REV. M. H. CLOSE, M.A., M.R.I.A.
COUNT PLUNKETT, B.L., M.R.I.A.

Hon. Secretaries.
RICHARD J. O'DUFFY.
BRIAN O'LOONEY, M.R.I.A., F.R.H.S.

Secretary of Council.
J. J. MACSWEENEY, R.I.A.

DUBLIN
6 MOLESWORTH STREET
1889.

MEMBERS OF COUNCIL.

Ali, Professor Mir Aulad, T.C.D.
Barry, Rev. Edmund, M.R.I.A., P.P., Rathcormac.
Bell, Hamilton, Esq., M.R.I.A., F.R.G.S.I.
Blackie, Professor, Edinburgh.
Close, Rev. M. H., M.A., Treasurer, Royal Irish Academy.
Conway, T. W., Esq., the Model Schools, Marlborough Street.
Corbet, W. J., Esq., M.P.
Cox, Michael F., Esq., M.D., M.R.I.A.
D'Arbois de Jubainville, Mons., Professor of Celtic in the College de France, Paris.
Dawson, Charles, Esq., T.C.
Dixon, Henry, Esq., Dublin.
Doherty, W. J., Esq., C.E., M.R.I.A.
Ernault, Mons. Emile, Poitiers.
Fitzgerald, Thomas, Esq., Ringsend.
Fitzgerald, The Most Rev. Wm., D.D., Bishop of Ross.
Goodman, Rev. James, M.A., T.C.D.
Halligan, James, Esq., Dublin.
Hart, C. H., Esq., A.B., Dublin.
Hennessy, Sir John Pope, K.C.M.G.
Holland, John, Esq., Ballinspital, Kinsale.
Lehane, D., Esq., Inspector of National Schools.
Lloyd, J. H., Esq., Dublin.
Lynch, Daniel, Esq., Dunleer.
MacCarthy, Rev. Professor Bartholomew, D.D., Todd Professor, Royal Irish Academy.
MacCarthy, Justin Huntly, Esq., M.P.
MacEnerney, Rev. F., C.C.
MacEniry, Major R., R.I.A.
MacSweeney, J. J., Esq., R.I.A.

MacSwiney, Rev. James, S.J.
MacTernan, Rev. S., P.P., M.R.I.A., Killasnett.
Moloney, M., Esq., Inspector, National Schools.
Murray, Æneas J., Esq., Head Master of the Model Schools, Cork.
Nettlau, Dr. Max, Vienna.
Nolan, Pierce L., Esq., B.A., Dublin.
O'Byrne, E., Esq., Tarn, France.
O'Byrne, Rev. L., C.C., Bray.
O'Byrne, Paul, Esq., Dublin.
O'Donel, C. J., Esq., J.P. M.R.I.A.
O'Duffy, R. J., Esq., Dublin.
O'Hanlon, Very Rev. John, Canon, P.P., M.R.I.A.
O'Hart, John, Esq., M.H.S.
O'Looney, Brian, Esq., M.R.I.A.
O'Meagher, J. C., Esq., M.R.I.A.
O'Reilly, Prof. J. P., M.R.I.A.
O'Riordan, T., Esq., Ringsend.
Plunkett, Count, B.L., M.R.I.A.
Rhys, Professor, Oxford University.
Rooney, Thomas, Esq., Dublin.
Ryan, L. J., Esq., Head Master Marlboro' Street Model Schools
Ryding, Dr. F., Merrion Square.
Schuchardt, Professor, University of Gratz, Styria.
Sexton, Right Hon. Thomas M.P., Lord Mayor.
Sigerson, George, Esq., M.D., M.R.I.A.
Sladen, Rev. R., P.P., Modeligo.
Sullivan, T. D., Esq., M.P., T.C.
Swan, Rev. Brother, Superior of Christian Schools, North Richmond Street, Dublin.
Ward, T., Esq., Dublin.
Zimmer, Dr. H., Greifswald, Prussia.

With power to add.

THIRD IRISH BOOK.

The chief object of this "Third Irish Book" is to enable the learner to think in Gaelic, and to express his thoughts in that language, presupposing, however, that he has already acquired a good knowledge of the First and Second Irish Books.

In order, then, to form sentences one must know the following at least, before proceeding further :—

  I. The verb ᴅo beiṫ, *to be.*

 II. The combinations of the various tenses of the verb ᴅo beiṫ, with the prepositional pronouns, which serve to express the ideas conveyed by the verbs *to have* and *to possess.*

III. Idioms, that is, modes of expression peculiar to the language. For instance :—
    1. Idioms arising from the special meanings attached to nouns or adjectives or prepositional pronouns in connection with the verb ᴅo beiṫ.
    2. Idioms of the adjective and noun.
    3.   „   Verb and nominative case.
    4.   „   Genitive case.
    5.   „   Demonstrative pronoun.

When the learner has mastered this book he will be able to enter on the study of the Declensions and Conjugations.

In the vocabularies at the head of the exercises, words which occur in the First or Second Books will not be repeated when used in the same sense. All terms used in this volume will, however, be given at the end. The literal English of each exercise will be found at the end of the book, and will form a series of exercises in translation of English sentences into Irish.

In accordance with the principle hitherto followed in these books, the exercises will be suited only to the subject of each part, but as the primary difficulties are disposed of, the exercises will be of a more general nature. In the next book the Declensions and Conjugations will be treated of, and the Irish pieces will be of greater length and more idiomatic, yet suited to learners who have carefully studied this and the preceding books.

PART I.

THE VERB ᴅo ḃeiṫ, *to be*.

The verb ᴅo ḃeiṫ, *to be* (pronounced *dhu veh*), is very full in Gaelic, having a variety of forms, expressive of existence, and of its relations to time, place, or thing.

In Section I. of this part, the various forms of the present tense of ᴅo ḃeiṫ shall be shown; in Section II. the forms of the past tense;

in Section III. the other moods and tenses. A table of the verb shall be given at the end of these exercises.

SECTION I.

FORMS OF THE PRESENT TENSE OF ᴅo ḃeiṫ.

Primary form,   tá   (*thaw.*)
Secondary or affected form, ꝼuil   (*fwil.*)
Assertive form, · iꞅ   (*iss.*)
Habitual form,   bíð, or bíðeann (*bee-an.*)

Two of these forms, namely, tá and iꞅ, are already familiar to the learner. Iꞅ, as already explained, is more definitely assertive in its meaning than tá. Iꞅ generally affirms or denotes existence, and is called the "Assertive Verb." Iꞅ is impersonal. Tá generally combines locality or condition with the fact of existence, and modifies the assertion by pointing out the time, place, or state of being.

After certain particles of inquiring, denying, &c., such as an, ní, naċ, ᵹo, the form ꝼuil (not tá or iꞅ) is employed in the present tense, and being modified by these particles in the manner explained in the *Second Book*, is seldom met without the eclipsing letter ḃ prefixed. It is the subjunctive mood of this verb, considered in some such form as that of interrogation or indirect relation.

bíöeann is termed the *habitual present tense*, and denotes a continuance of existence in a certain state not unlike the form "I do be," or, "I am in the habit of being," which is sometimes heard in English.

Each of these forms of the present tense has its respective form in the past tense. Each form may be used without any change in connection with singular and plural numbers either of nouns or pronouns. Tá, ꞅuil, and bíöeann have also another form, in which the pronoun is incorporated with the verb, so as to make with it a single word. In the first exercises, the simpler form only shall be given, in which the pronouns are expressed separately, as in the following

EXAMPLES.

	Singular.			Plural.	
tá, ꞅuil, bíöeann,	}	{ mé. tú. ꞅé, ꞅí.	tá, ꞅuil, bíöeann,	}	{ ꞅinn. ꞅib. ꞅiad.
iꞅ	{ mé. tú, tú. ꞅé, é. ꞅí, í.		iꞅ	{ ꞅinn, inn. ꞅib, ib, ꞅiad, iad.	

OBSERVE.—In the above examples, the pronouns, which are nominatives to tá, &c., do not precede, but follow the verb. (See *First Book*, p. 15.) Thus the English "I am" is in Irish "am I," like the not unusual forms "say I," "say we," "quoth he," &c.

PRESENT TENSE.

In connection with the verb ιγ, the secondary or affected forms of the pronouns are often used, particularly in the third person.

In this work the primary forms ɼınn, ɼıb, &c., shall be employed. However, when a word or words intervenes between ιγ and the pronoun the affected forms are used, as in the phrase ιγ mɑιċ ɑn ɼeɑp é, He is a good man. This is conformable to general usage and pronunciation, but is sometimes not followed in the first and second persons of the plural.

These forms are known as the accusative case of the pronouns, and as such are employed when the pronoun is the object of the verb, as ʋo buɑıl ɼé é, he struck him—see Second Book, Note, p. 55. In phrases like ιγ mɑιċ ɑn ɼeɑp é, é is not nominative case to ιγ.

EXERCISE I.

The Forms cá and b-ɸuıl.

Present Tense—Primary Form.

Singular.	Plural.
1. cá mé, I am.	1. cá ɼınn, we are.
2. cá cú, thou art.	2. cá ɼıb, you are.
3. cá { ré, he is. / rí, she is.	3. cá ɼıɑʋ, they are.

Same Tense—Secondary Form.

1. b-ɸuıl mé? am I?	b-ɸuıl ɼınn? are we.
2. b-ɸuıl cú? art thou?	b-ɸuıl ɼıb? are you.
3. b-ɸuıl { ré, is he? / rí, is she?	b-ɸuıl ɼıɑʋ? are they?

The secondary form of the present tense of the verb *to be* is shown thus:—

"I am," simply, is in Gaelic tá mé; but "he says *that I am*," is rendered into Gaelic by "ḋeiṗ ṗé ʒo b-ḟuil mé"—it is not ḋeiṗ ṗé ʒo ḋ-tá mé. Tá is only used in the direct present; and b-ḟuil is employed when the verb (to be) follows another verb on which it is dependent, or when a question is asked, or a wish expressed, or something denied; as, (an) b-ḟuil tú ṗlán, "art thou well," is the same as "I ask art thou well"—(ḟiaḟṗuiʒim) an b-ḟuil tú ṗlán. B-ḟuil is also used when preceded by a relative pronoun governed by a preposition, or signifying "all which."

OBSERVE.—Verbs have a special form in use after the relative pronouns. There is no such form in the verb "ḋo beiṫ" except in the future tense, which is beiḋeaṗ and buṗ, which shall be shown. biḋeaṗ is often heard in the relative form of the habitual present; as an té a biḋeaṗ, *he who does be;* but biḋeaiin is also used, as, an té naċ m-biḋeann, *he who does not be.* Tá and bí are used after a. Noċ generally precedes the form iṗ and sometimes the past tense.

The learner will remember that the relative pronoun a, expressed or understood, aspirates the initial of the following word.

b-ḟuil tú ṗlán is used as a contracted form of an b-ḟuil tú ṗlán. An, *whether*, in short sentences and in conversation is usually omitted. It cannot be well omitted in other verbs which have no special interrogative or negative form. An, *whether*, causes eclipsis, ní, *not*, aspiration. There are, however, in the writings of Mr. Hardiman, Dr. MacHale, and others, and in the spoken language of the people, many instances in which the soft *w* sound of b-ḟuil (*will*) is retained after ní rather than the contracted form ní'l (*is not*) or ní ḟuil, in which ḟ is com-

pletely quiescent, and a hiatus is produced between n'
and ḟuıl (*nee'ill.*)

NOTE.—The affected form of regular verbs would be shown by the initial letter (where possible) being eclipsed by the particles going before. In ꝺo beıċ, however, instead of eclipsing the initial of tá in these cases, a special form, ꝼuıl, is employed, which is eclipsed by these particles.

EXERCISE II.

a, who, whom.
ꝺeıp, says.

ní, not.
po-ṡeaꞃ, very pretty.

1. An b-ꝼuıl tú ꝑlán? 2. Ní b-ꝼuıl mé tınn. 3. Ní ḟuıl an mac óg, acṫ tá ꞃé ꝑlán. 4. Iꞃ ꞃé ꞃo an ꝼeaꞃ ag a b-ꝼuıl an cú móꞃ.* 5. An ꝼeaꞃ aguꞃ an bean aguꞃ an mac óg, an b-ꝼuıl ꞃıaꝺ ꝑlán? 6. Tá ꞃıaꝺ ꝑlán, acṫ ní b-ꝼuıl ꞃıaꝺ óg no áꞃꝺ. 7. Ꝺeıꞃ ꞃé go b-ꝼuıl mé óg ꝼóꞃ. 8. Muna b-ꝼuıl tú maıṫ, ní b-ꝼuıl tú ꞃeunṁaꞃ. 9. An b-ꝼuıl an bean ꝺeaꞃ? 10. Tá ꞃí ꝑó-ṡeaꞃ aguꞃ ıꞃ maıṫ an bean í.

EXERCISE III.

Ꝺıaꞃmuıꝺ, Dermot Loꞃcan, Lorcan (Laurence.)

* " He is the man at whom is (who has) the big hound." This idiom is already familiar to the learner, but shall be fully explained in the succeeding section. The use of tá and ıꞃ in reference to possession, is also well known.

THE VERB do beiṫ.

naċ, who not, which not.

1. An b-ḟuil an lá ḟada? 2. Tá an lá ḟada. 3. Deir Taḋg naċ b-ḟuil an lá ḟada. 4. Deir Diarmuid go b-ḟuil an lá ḟada. 5. B-ḟuil tú cinnte go b-ḟuil an lá ḟada? 6. Tá mé cinnte go b-ḟuil an lá ḟada. 7. B-ḟuil an mac óg agur b-ḟuil ré plán agur ara? 8. Tá an mac óg agur tá ré plán, aċt ní ḟuil ré ara. 9. B-ḟuil do ċapa, Lorcan, rionn agur ara—mór agur plán? 10. Tá ré rionn agur ara—óg agur mór, aċt ní b-ḟuil ré plán.

Exercise IV.

The forms ir and tá.

Ir mé, it is I.   Ir rinn, inn, it is we.
Ir tú, it is thou.   Ir rib, ib, it is you.
Ir ré, é, it is he.   Ir rad, iad, it is they.
Ir rí, í, it is she.

criona, prudent.   úṁal, humble.
Murċaḋ, Morrogh, Morty.

1. Ir ḟear boċt brian agur tá ré plán 2. Ir ḟear raiḋbir Murċaḋ aċt ní ḟuil ré plán. 3. Ir ḟear óg mire agur tá mé úṁal. 4. Ir maiṫ an rgeul rin go deiṁin. 5. Ir ḟear láidir Tomár, agur tá ré plán. 6. Tá Nóra boċt, aċt ir rí a tá criona. 7. Tá Peadar agur Pádraic mór, aċt ní b-ḟuil rad glic.

PRESENT TENSE.

8. 'Sé ʋo beaċa; an cupa a cá ann? 9. Iꞃ me a cá ann ꞃo; iꞃ ꝼíoꞃ ꝣo b-ꝼuil mé ann ꞃo. 10. Ꝣꞃáʋ mo ċꞃoiʋe ċú

Observe in the foregoing sentences the use of iꞃ, as contrasted with ca. Iꞃ is never used after the relative pronoun a (See No. 6, cá nóꞃa boċc, aċc iꞃ ꞃí a cá cꞃíona.).

The learner is aware that the secondary or accusative forms of the pronouns are more generally employed in connection with the verb iꞃ, especially in the third person singular and plural. iꞃ ꞃé, iꞃ ꞃí, iꞃ iaʋ, are frequently written 'ꞃé, it is he, 'ꞃí, it is she, 'ꞃiaʋ, it is they, and often without an apostrophe.

Examples.

Iꞃ mé. It is I. (It is I, and no other.) Iꞃ ꝼíoꞃ ꞃin. That is true (it is true, that), (that *at least* is true.)

Iꞃ ꞃeaꞃ óꝣ é. He is a young man. Iꞃ óꝣ an ꞃeaꞃ é. (Is young, the man, he.)

The form iꞃ is employed:—

1. When in English the pronoun "it," would come before " is ;" as iꞃ ꞃé a cá ann, it is he who is there.

2. When the demonstrative pronouns ꞃo "this" and ꞃin "that" are employed as nominatives (without a noun); as iꞃ ꞃé ꞃo, it is this, &c.

3. Generally when an assertion is made which admits no idea of doubt (or condition

as to locality), or when in case of contrast one is selected before others. Hence, ıṗ is used to point out the comparative and superlative of adjectives, because contrast is pointed out with certainty ; as níoṗ (i.e. níȯ iṗ) ḟeáṗṗ, iṗ ḟeáṗṗ.

The remarks also apply to buḋ, the form of the perfect, and buṗ, of the future, which correspond to iṗ.

EXERCISE V.

The forms tá and bíḋeann.

bíḋeann mé, bíȯ mé. bíḋeann ṗinn, bíȯ ṗinn.
bíḋeann tú, bíȯ tú. bíḋeann ṗib, bíȯ ṗib.
bíḋeann ṗé, bíȯ ṗé. bíḋeann ṗiao, bíȯ ṗiao.

a ġ-cóṁnuiḋe, always. oe ġnát, usually. ?
bṗeoite, ailing, sick. ṗoiġioeaċ, patient.
oeaṗbṗáitṗe, brothers. ṗeaċtṁain, a week.

1. Bíḋeann tú ann ṗúo ġo minic. 2. Ḋeiṗ Taḋġ ġo m-bíḋeann ṗiao annṗ an m-baile ġaċ lá. 3. Ní b-ḟuil ṗé ann, aċt bíḋeann ṗé annṗ an tiġ ṗin ġaċ ṗeaċtṁain. 4. An m-bíḋeann tú ṗlán ? 5. Bíḋeann ṗláinte ṁait aġam oe ġnát, buiḋeaċaṗ le Ḋia. 6. Ní bíḋeann ṗiao ṗlán a ġ-cóṁnuiḋe. 7. Iṗ

OBS.—The termination eann in this and other verbs denotes continuance of action.

feap paiöbip é anoip agup tá ré pal, map bióeann a óeappáitpe. 8. Tá tú tinn anoip act ní bióeann tú bpeoite. 9. bióeann áó aip amaóán. 10. Má bióeann tú boct, bí poigióeaċ.

Exercise VI.

The assertive verb ip is omitted in asking questions with the particles an *whether*, and naċ, *whether not*, and after the negative particle. The other forms of óo beit are expressed when used in such cases.

OBS.—In this case, as usual, ip may be considered in some sense a separate verb, so like tá, it has its primary and secondary forms; the latter being shown by the particle and the omission of the verb.

1. An mé, an tú, an é? 2. Ní pnn, ní pb, ní h-iaó. 3. Naċ é, naċ í, naċ iaó? 4. An tú a tá ann? 5. Ip tú a tá ann. 6. Naċ bpeág an óuine mé? 7. Ní olc an peap tú. 8. Naċ bpeág na pip iaó? 9. Ip piaó a tá ann. 10. Naċ óeap an bean í?

OBS.—The words tá ann, *is in it*, mean *in life* or existing, or present in a special place, as when friends meet; as, an tú a tá ann, Is it you who are in it? &c.

The secondary forms of the personal pronouns which are used with the verb ip are generally employed in the cases above referred to: a h is prefixed for Euphony in such cases as ní h-iaó, &c.

THE VERB do beiṫ.

Exercise VII.

díreać, sure, straight.
díoġalṫas, vengeance.
ɼo mall, slowly (late).
maiṫ, a good, goodness.
stuaim, prudence, modesty

1. Naċ breáġ an lá é ɼo? 2. Iʀ breáġ an lá é ɼo deiṁin. 3. Iʀ breáġ an ṁaidin í ɼo. 4. Iʀ rearɼ maiṫ dman, iʀ bean ṁaiṫ Máire. 5. Iʀ reáɼɼ go mall ioná go bráṫ.* 6. Má'ʀ mall iʀ díreać díoġalṫas Dé. 7. Iʀ reáɼɼ stuaim ioná neaɼṫ. 8. Iʀ reáɼɼ an ṁaiṫ a ṫá ioná an ṁaiṫ a bí. 9. Deiɼ tú guɼ reáɼɼ an ṁaiṫ a ṫá ioná an ṁaiṫ a bí. 10. Deiɼ mé réin guɼ breáġ an lá é ɼo.

Obs.—guɼ in the foregoing sentences is not the form of go, which is used with the past tense, but is for guɼ ab, a subjunctive form of iɼ, with ab understood.

Exercise VIII.

Examples of the Synthetic Present Tense.

As before remarked, ṫá, b-ɼuil and bíoeann have each a form different from that treated of in the preceding exercises. This is called the *synthetic form*, because the nominative case *when a pronoun* is joined to the verb and forms with it one word, as in the following

* go bráṫ here means *never*.

PRESENT TENSE.

Examples.

cáim,	tá mé.	támaoid, tá ɲınn.
táiɲ,	tá tú.	tátaoi, tá ɲıb
tá ɲé, ɲí.		táid,	tá ɲıad.
b-ꝼuilim,	b-ꝼuil mé.	b-ꝼuilmíd,b-ꝼuil ɲınn.
b-ꝼuiliɲ,	b-ꝼuil tú.	b-ꝼuilti, b-ꝼuil ɲıb.
b-ꝼuil ɲé, ɲí.		b-ꝼuilid, b-ꝼuil ɲıad.
bıóim,	bıóeann mé.	bıómíd,	bıóeann ɲınn
bıóiɲ,	bıóeann tú.	bıótí,	bıóeann ɲıb.
bıó (or bıóeann), ɲé, ɲí.		bıóid,	bıóeann ɲıad.

OBS.—The latter form here given in each case is familiar to the learner. It is not necessary, therefore, to give the English of these examples as both forms have the same meaning.

The second form (in which the verb does not change its termination for the different persons) is called the *analytic form*, because the pronouns stand separate from the verb.

The first form is the more classic, but both are in constant use. A distinction is sometimes made in interrogative phrases by using the analytic form, i.e., the form in which the pronouns are expressed separately, and in which the verb does not change in termination, for asking questions; and the synthetic form for replying. In the South the synthetic form is the more generally in use.

The learner will remark that the third person singular has but one form, which is the same as that used in all the persons of the analytic process.

iꞅ, as already explained, has but one form.

EXERCISE IX.

a'ꞅ (contracted form of aʒuꞅ) as, and.
coṁ (or ċo) so, as.
ne, an emphatic suffix.

'ꞅa (contracted form of annꞅ an), in the.
ꞅláinteaṁail, healthy

THE VERB DO beıc.

1. b-ꝼuil tú a pláınte maıt? 2. Táım₁ buırdeacar le Dıa. 3. Deıp ré nac b-ꝼuılım plán. 4. bıóım 'ꞃa m-baıle gac lá. 5. An m-bıdeann na pıp buanꞃaoġalac annꞃ an áıt pın? 6. bıóıo go deımın act ní bıóıo com pláınteamáıl a'ꞃ támaoıd-ne. 7. Muna b-ꝼuılmíd com ꞃaıóbıp a'ꞃ táıd. 8. bıótí annꞃ an g-catıaıp pın go mınıc. 9. bıómíd go mınıc ann púd. 10. Tátaoı bott, act ıꞃ ꜱlıc na pıp ꞃıb.

Exercise X.

a n-dé, yesterday.   cnoıc, hills.
a n-dıu, to-day.   ꝼeuꞃmaꞃ, grassy.

1. Nac bꞃeáġ an oıdce í ꞃo? 2. Deıp bꞃıan go m-bud bꞃeaġ an lá an lá a n-dé, aꝛuꞃ ꜱuꞃ lá bꞃeáġ an lá a n-dıu. 3. Iꞃ ꜱlaꞃ ıad na cnoıc a b-ꝼad uaınn. 4. Má'ꞃ ꜱlaꞃ ıad, ní ꝼeuꞃmaꞃ. 5. Nac ꝼóꜱlumta an ꝼeaꞃ é bꞃıan. 6. Iꞃ ꞃcolaıꞃe clıꞃte é go deımın. 7. Támaoıd aꜱ ꝼóꜱluım ꜱaedıl ꜱe. 8. Tátaoı aꜱ deunad go maıt. 9. bıómíd aꜱ léıꜱead an céıd leabaıꞃ aꝛuꞃ an daꞃa leabaıꞃ aꜱ an ꞃcoıl ann a b-ꝼuılmíd. 10. Iꞃ maıt an ꞃꜱeul é ꞃın.

NOTE.—bud often causes aspiration of the initial of the word which follows it.

SECTION II.

FORMS OF THE PAST TENSE OF ᴅo ḃeiṫ.

Primary form,	ḃi	(*vee.*)
Secondary form,	ṗaiḃ	(*rev.*)
Assertive form,	buḋ	(*bu.*)
Habitual form,	ḃiḋeaḋ	(*vee-ach.*)

Ḃi, ṗaiḃ, ḃiḋeaḋ, and buḋ, in the past tense correspond respectively to ᴛá, ḃ-ꜰuil, biḋeann and iꜱ in the present tense, and follow the same rules which have been just explained. The first three have also a synthetic as well as an analytic form, both of which shall be shown. Buḋ, like iꜱ, has but one form :—

Examples.

ḃi } { mé.
ṗaiḃ } { ᴛú.
ḃiḋeaḋ } { ꜱé, ꜱi,

ḃi. } { ꜱinn.
ṗaiḃ } { ꜱiḃ.
ḃiḋeaḋ. } { ꜱiaᴅ.

buḋ { mé.
ᴛú, ṫú.
ꜱé, h-é.
ꜱi, h-i.

buḋ { ꜱinn, inn.
ꜱiḃ, iḃ.
ꜱiaᴅ, h-iaᴅ.

THE VERB do beiṫ.

Exercise I.

bí and paıb.

Singular.

bı mé, I was,
bí tú, thou wast.
bí { ré, he was
     { rí, she was.

Plural.

bí rınn, we were.
bí rıb, ye were.
bí rıad, they were.

paıb mé, was I?
paıb tú, wast thou?
paıb { ré, was he?
       { rí, was she?

paıb rınn, were we?
paıb rıb, were ye?
paıb rıad were they.

Exercise II.

1. bí mé annr an g-cataıp a n-dıu. 2. Raıb tú ag an g-cappaıg? 3. Ní paıb mé fór ann 4. An paıb an mac óg? 5. Deıp ré go paıb tú maıt. 6. bí ré raıdbıp aċt ní paıb ré maıt. 7. Deıp Tadg naċ paıb rıad boċt 8. Muna paıb tú láıdıp, do bí tú glıc. 9 Táım cınnte naċ paıb rí mapb. 10. bí ré raop.

Obs.—bí often takes do, the sign of the perfect tense before it. Raıb does not, as po, another sign of the same tense, is incorporated with it; that is po bı. So an and ní are used rather than ap and noıp before paıb

PAST TENSE.

OBS.—buð in negative and interrogative sentences, such s níoṗ me, ⱭṖ mé, &c., above, is often omitted. (See notes n 1ꞃ p. 11.)

NOTE—When the distinctive particle is not expressed efore b-ꞃuıL or ṗⱭıb, the sentence is understood to be inerrogative.

EXERCISE III.

Examples of other forms.

bıṁeⱭṁ and buṁ.

ıṁeⱭṁ mé, I used to be.   bıṁeⱭṁ ṗınn, we used
ıṁeⱭṁ ċú, thou usedst   to be.
   to be.   bıṁeⱭṁ ṗıb, ye used to
ıṁeⱭṁ ꞃé, { he } used   be.
     ꞃı, { she } to be. bıṁeⱭṁ ṗⱭⱱ, They
                       used to be.

uṁ mé, it was I.   buṁ ṗınn, ınn, it was we.
uṁ ċú, ċú, it was thou.   buṁ ṗıb, ıb, it was ye.
uṁ ꞃé, é, it was he.   buṁ ṗⱭⱱ, h-Ɑⱱ, it was
uṁ ꞃı, ı, it was she.   they.

EXERCISE IV.

ꞃoın, since that.   nⱭṗ, that not, that may
Ɑⱱ ó ꞃoın, long ago.   not.

1. Ḃi mé Ɑ n-ⱱıu Ɑ n-Ɑıċ ⱱo bıṁeⱭṁ mé
b-ꞃⱭⱱ ó ꞃoın. 2. buṁ ṗⱭⱱ nⱭ ꞃıṗ Ɑ ḃi Ɑıṗ Ɑn
-ṗṖⱭıⱱ Ɑn ċ-Ɑm ṗın. 3. Ɑṗ mé Ɑn ꞃeⱭṗ

THE VERB DO beit.

a bróeaḋ ann? 4. Níop mé an fear. 5. An m-bróeaḋ mé ann? 6. Ní bróeaḋ tú ve ẓnáṫ ann. 7. Ap pb a bróeaḋ ann faḋ ó fom? 8. Nap tú féin a bróeaḋ ann? 9. Níop mé ẓo veiṁin. 10. Nap buḋ fé. Ẓo m-buḋ plán tú.

OBS.—buḋ in such sentences as the above is omitted, as ap me, for ap buḋ mé? was it I—and níop mé, for níop buḋ mé, it was not I. (See remarks on ir, p. 11.)

OBS.—buḋ frequently aspirates the initial of the following word. It aspirates the initials of the pronouns, particularly the third person, which accompany it, and which are generally written with h prefixed (instead of the aspirated ṗ), as buḋ h-é, h-í, &c., and sometimes in the accusative form. When a word or words intervenes between buḋ and the pronoun, the secondary form of the pronoun is used; as buḋ ṁait an fear é, he was a good man. (See notes on ir, p. 5.)

The ṗ (*aspirated* p) shall in such cases be prefixed in these books rather than h.

OBS.—Náp mé, was it not I? is the form of the perfect tense (buḋ omitted). But náp buḋ is also in use. The words mean "may it not be"—buḋ expressed is in that position optative, or subjunctive; as náp buḋ faḋa buan-raoẓalaċ tú, that thou mayest not be enduring, long-lived.

NOTE.—Ap is composed of an, whether, and po, sign of the perfect indicative. náp = naċ (present interrogative negative) and po = naċp = náp; níop = ní and po, ẓup = ẓo that and po; munap is from má if, ní not, and po, sign of perfect tense.

EXERCISE V.

cabaip, help.
oliẓe, law.
ẓioppa, nearer (from ẓeapp short.)

✗ piaċtanap, necessity.
ran, an emphatic suffix.

* Ẓo m-buḋ signifies "that it may be."

PAST TENSE.

1. Ir ṡioppa cabaiṗ Dé 'ná an voṗar. 2. Duḃ ḃreáġ an lá, an lá a n-vé. 3. An iav a tá ann? 4. Ní h-iav na ṗiṗ aċt ir ṗiav na mná a ḃí ann. 5. Támaoiv óġ aġuṗ ṗlán aċt táiv-ran raiḃḃiṗ. 6. Ní ḃ-ṗuil vliġe aġ ṗiaċtanaṗ. 7. Ní ḃíveaṫ ṗinn maṗ ṗo. 8. Ḃiḃim a ṗláinte ṁait, buiveaċaṗ le Dia. 9. Ní ḃ-ṗuiliv tinn anoiṗ aċt táiv laġ ṗóṗ. 10. Táṫaoi óġ aġuṗ láiviṗ.

Exercise VI.

Examples of the synthetic Past Tense:

ḃíveaṗ, ḃí mé.	ḃíveamaṗ, ḃí ṗinn.
ḃíviṗ, ḃí tú.	ḃíveaḃaṗ, ḃí ṗiḃ.
ḃí ṗé, ṗí.	ḃíveavaṗ, ḃí ṗiav.
ṗaḃaṗ, ṗaiḃ mé.	ṗaḃamaṗ, ṗaiḃ ṗinn.
ṗaḃaiṗ, ṗaiḃ tú.	ṗaḃaḃaṗ, ṗaiḃ ṗiḃ.
ṗaiḃ ṗé, ṗí.	ṗaḃavaṗ, ṗaiḃ ṗiav.
ḃíḃinn, ḃíveaṫ mé.	ḃíḃmiṗ, ḃíveaṫ ṗinn
ḃíṫeá, ḃíveaṫ tú.	ḃíṫí, ḃíveaṫ ṗiḃ.
ḃíveaṫ ṗé, ṗí.	ḃíviṗ, ḃíveaṫ ṗiav.

The second form in each case is the analytic, and is already familiar. The synthetic past tense (primary form) is also written—

1. ḃíoṗ,   ḃíomaṗ.
2. ḃíṗ,   ḃíoḃaṗ.
3. ḃí ṗé,   ḃíovaṗ.

Exercise VII.

ꝼᴀᴅ ó, long since.   ᴣo leoꞃ, enough.
ꝼáᴣ (ᴅ'ꝼáᴣ *past*.) left.

1. An ꞃᴀbᴀıꞃ ᴀᴣ ᴀn ᴣ-cᴀꞃꞃᴀıᴣ? 2. Ní ꞃᴀbᴀꞃ ꝼéın ᴀᴣ ᴀn ᴣ-cᴀꞃꞃᴀıᴣ ᴣıᴅ ᴣo m-bıᴅeᴀú mo ṁuınᴄıꞃ ᴀnnꞃ ᴀn áıᴄ ꞃın ᴀ n-ᴀm ꝼᴀᴅ ó. 3. An m-bíᴅíꞃ ᴀnn ꞃúᴅ ᴅe ᴣnáᴄ? 4. Ɖeıꞃ ꞃé ᴣo ꞃᴀbᴀᴅᴀꞃ óᴣ. 5. Ꙃo ꞃᴀıb ᴄú ꞃláɴ ᴀᴣuꞃ ᴣo m-buᴅ buᴀn ᴄú. 6. Ɖo bıᴅeᴀᴅᴀꞃ ꞃláɴ ᴀᴄᴄ ní ꞃᴀbᴀᴅᴀꞃ ꞃᴀıᴅbıꞃ. 7. Ní bıᴅınn ꞃláɴ ó ᴅ'ꝼáᴣ mé mo ᴄíꞃ ꝼéın. 8. Ƃıᴅᴄeá ᴀᴣ ᴅul ó bᴀıle ᴣo bᴀıle. 9. Iꞃ ꝼíoꞃ ꞃın ᴣo ᴅeıꞃın, ᴀᴄᴄ ní ꞃᴀbᴀꞃ ꝼóꞃ ᴀ n-áıᴄ mᴀꞃ ᴀn áıᴄ ꞃo. 10. Ɲᴀᴄ m-bıᴅᴄı ꞃᴀıᴅbıꞃ ᴣo leoꞃ ᴀn ᴄᴀn ꞃın.

Exercise VIII.

ᴀnlᴀn, a condiment.
"Kitchen," anything eaten as a relish with food.
bonn, a groat.
boꞃb, fierce, haughty (a haughty person).
bıᴅeᴀnn boꞃb ꞃᴀoı ꞃᴣéıṁ "the haughty (one), is often under (the form of) beauty."
cáıꞃᴅe, respite, time (for payment).
coꞃꞃ ᴀıꞃ cáıꞃᴅe, means a crane not yet caught.
ceo, a mist.
coꞃꞃ, a crane.
cúıꞃᴄ, a court.

ᴅıoṁᴀoın, idle.
ᴅꞃeoılın, a wren.
ꝼáıᴅ, a prophet.
ᴣnóᴄᴀᴄ, busy.
ᴅꞃoᴄ-ᴣnóᴄᴀᴄ, badly employed.
ımꞃeᴀꞃ, strife. X
ꞃáᴅ, a saying.
'ꞃᴀ (ᴀnnꞃ ᴀn), in the.
ꞃᴣéıṁ, beauty.
ꞃꞃᴀꞃáɴ, a purse.
ꞃúıle, eyes.
ᴄᴀn, time.
uᴀıᴣneᴀꞃ, solitude.

PAST TENSE.

1. Raib a ceann liat? 2. Ní paib a ceann liat an t-am ʄin act tá ré liat anoiʄ. 3. b-ʄuil a ʄúile goʄim? 4. Ní b-ʄuilio, act táid donn. 5. Táiʄ plán anoiʄ, aguʄ go m-buó ʄada maʄ ʄin tú. 6. buó ʄeaʄ mait é, act ní h-é an ʄeaʄ aiʄ a b-ʄuil meaʄ. 7. An ʄababaʄ ʄaoi meaʄ annʄ an tiʄ ʄo? 8. Ní ʄabamaʄ, óiʄ ní b-ʄuil meaʄ aiʄ an b-ʄáid ann a tiʄ ʄéin. 9. Iʄ ʄioʄ an ʄáo é ʄin go deiṁin. 10. bidinn ʄaióbiʄ an tan ʄin aguʄ biotéá bott annʄ an am ceudna. 11. Ní b-ʄuil ʄóg gan anʄóg. 12. Iʄ ʄeaʄʄ beit diomaoin ioná oʄocgnótac. 13. Iʄ ʄeaʄʄ impeaʄ ioná uaigneaʄ. 14. bideann boʄb ʄaoi ʄgéim. 15. bideann áó aiʄ amadán. 16. Ní b-ʄuil annʄ an t-ʄaogal ʄo act ceo. 17. Ní buan cogaó na g-caʄiad. 18. Ní bideann tʄeun buan. 19. Má táim bott tá cʄioide ʄial agam. 20. Iʄ mait an t-anlan an t-ocʄaʄ. 21. Aʄ b'é ʄin an ʄeaʄ a bí tinn? 22. Deiʄ ʄiad go ʄaib ʄé, act ní h-é an ʄeaʄ tinn anoiʄ é. 23. An té bideann diomaoin, bideann ʄé oʄoc-gnótac. 24. Iʄ ʄeaʄʄ, caʄa 'ʄa g-cúiʄt, ioná bonn 'ʄa ʄpaʄán. 25 ʄeaʄʄ oʄeoilín a n-doʄn, ioná coʄʄ aiʄ cáiʄde.

OBS.—Adjectives are sometimes used as nouns, as boʄb, a haughty (person), and tʄéun (the) valiant, in above examples.

SECTION III.

MOODS AND TENSES OF ᴅo ʙeɪᴛ—*(continued.)*

The learner has now seen all the forms of the present and past tenses of the indicative mood of ᴅo ʙeɪᴛ and those secondary forms which always follow certain particles and may be considered as subjunctive. We shall now treat of the future tense of ᴅo ʙeɪᴛ, thus finishing the indicative, which is the principal mood, the other moods having but one tense and one form for each.

The future tense has but one form for primary and secondary meaning, or direct and indirect narration; beıᴅ c bıáıᴅ (*will be*), is the analytic form, which after relative pro nouns becomes beıᴅeáp, and does not change.

beıᴅeáᴅ, &c., is the synthetic form.

EXERCISE I.

The future tense of ᴅo ʙeɪᴛ.

Examples.

beıᴅeáᴅ, beıᴅ mé, I will be. beıᴅmíᴅ, beıᴅ pınn, we will be.

beıᴅıp, beıᴅ ᴛú, thou wilt be. beıᴅíᴅ, beıᴅ pıb, you will be.

beıᴅ pé, pí, he (or she) will be. beıᴅıᴅ, beıᴅ pıaᴅ, they will be.

Relative form ᴀ beıᴅeáp, who will be.

ʙup, it will be, is the future of ıp.

FUTURE TENSE.

bur is seldom employed except before adjectives in the superlative degree with a contingent or future meaning. It is sometimes spelled buḋ and bıḋ.

OBS.—The initial of beıḋ is subject to aspiration and eclipsis, as in Rule X. (part I.), and Rule V. (part II.), of "Second Irish Book."

EXERCISE II.

aṫṗuġaḋ, a change, removal.
aṫṗuġaḋ a máṗać, after to-morrow; aṫṗuġaḋ a ṗéıṗ, the night before last.
ćuġaınn, towards us.
an t-ṗeaćtṁaın ṗo ćuġaınn, this week towards us, i.e., next week.
Ġaıllıṁ, Galway.

ġo ḋ-tí, until.
Luımneać,) Lime-
Luımnıġ (dat.),) rick.
ṗéıṗ, i.e., a ṗéıṗ, last night.
ṗa, an emphatic suffix.
uaṗaıl (dat. fem.), noble.

1. Beıḋeaḋ a Luımnıġ a máṗać. 2. Ní beıḋ mé ann ṗın ġo ḋ-tí aṫṗuġaḋ a máṗać, aćt bí mo ḋeaṗḃṗátaıṗ ann aṫṗuġaḋ a ṗéıṗ. 3. Ḋeıṗ ṗé naċ m-beıḋ ṗıaḋ annṗ an tıġ. 4. Beıḋıḋ annṗ an tıġ ṗın ġo cınnte, aġuṗ beıḋ-eaḋ-ṗa annṗ an tıġ eıle. 5. Iṗ ṗé ṗın an ḟeaṗ a beıḋeaṗ aġ ḋul ġo Ġaıllıṁ an t-ṗeaċtṁaın ṗo ćuġaınn. 6. Beıḋmíḋ móṗ ṗóṗ. 7. Beıḋ an Ġaeḋılġe ṗaoı ṁeaṗ ṗóṗ, ı n-Éıṗınn uaṗaıl, ı n-ınıṗ na ṗıġ. 8. An m-beıḋ tú aġ ḋul ġuṗ an ḃ-ṗaıṗıġe? 9. Beıḋeaḋ. 10. Beıḋıṗ áṗḋ aġuṗ móṗ aġuṗ ṗlán.

Exercise III.

The Conditional Mood of do beiṫ.

Examples.

beiḋinn, beiḋeaḋ mé, I would be.
beiḋteá, thou wouldst be.
beiḋeaḋ sé, sí, he (or she) would be.
beiḋmíf, beiḋeaḋ sinn, we would be.
beiḋtí, beiḋeaḋ siḃ, ye would be.
beidíf, beiḋeaḋ siad, they would be.

baḋ is the conditional of is; as, dá m-baḋ mé, if it were I.

Obs.—These are the only forms of the Conditional Mood. The particle do is used before it, and even where not expressed, causes aspiration of the initial, as above. Dá, if, is very frequently used with it, and sometimes muna, unless, both of which cause eclipsis; as, dá m-beiḋinn, if I should be.

Exercise IV.

a ḃaile, at home (to) home.
dob' (do buḋ), it was.
réiḋ, ready.
síotċáin, peace.

1. Beiḋmís a b-fad ó'n t-saoġal. 2. Deis sé go m-beiḋeaḋ sé fásda leis. 3. Ní beiḋteá réiḋ faoi an am sin. 4. Muna m-beiḋinn, dob' féidis duit siúbal leat féin. 5. Dá m-baḋ toil liom sin a ḋeunaḋ, dob' féidis nacas b' áil leat é sin. 6. Dá m-beidís saor, do beiḋeaḋ siad fásda go leor. 7. Dá

m-beiṫeaḋ aiṗṡeaḋ aṡam-ṗa, beiṫeaḋ ṗé aṡaṫ-ṗa maṗi an ṡ-ceuḋna. 8. Muna m-beiṫeaḋ an niḋ ṗo aṁáin ḋo beiṫómiṗ a ṗioṫṫáin annṗ an am ṗo. 9. Ḋo beiṫómiṗ a baile a b-ṗaḋ ó ṫoin. 10. Ḋo beiṫóṫí ann ṗin ṡo cinnṫe.

Exercise V.

The Imperative Mood of ḋo beiṫ.

Examples.

bí, be thou.
bíṫeaḋ ṗé, ṗí, let him (or her) be.

bímiṗ (biom), let us be.
biḋiḋ, be ye.
bíḋiṗ, be they, let them be.

Obs.—As in other languages, the Imperative Mood has no first person singular. The second person singular of this Mood, (bí, be thou), is, in ḋo beiṫ, and every other Irish verb, the root from which all the other moods, tenses, and persons are formed, by the addition of certain inflected endings. It is the simplest part of the verb, and has no analytic form. We could not use, as in other instances, bíṫeaḋ ṫú, for bí, be thou.

Exercise VI.

aṗ ṗo, from this, hence.
bṗónaċ, sorrowful.
cṗuaiḋ, hard.
ṡníoṁ, an act.

ṡníoṁaṗṫaib (*dat.pl*)
acts.
ṗúṡaċ, merry.
ṫeanṡa, a tongue.
ṫeanṡain (*dat.*)

26 THE VERB oo beiṫ.

1. Ná bí cruaiḋ aġur ná bí boġ. 2. Ná bíḋeaḋ eaġla orc. 3. Ná bíḋeaḋ náire oraib. 4. Ná bíḋeaḋ oo ġníoṁ ó oo ċeanġain. 5. Bí rároa leir rin. 6. Biṁir aġ oul ar ro. 7. Bí cnearoa ann oo ġníoṁarċaib. 8. Biṁir ġo rúġaċ, aġur ná bíḋiḋ brónaċ. 9. Bíḋeaḋ rior aġaib ġo b-ruil rin ceart. 10. Bíḋeaḋ ré raori.

EXERCISE VII.
Infinitive Mood and participles of oo beiṫ.

oo, or a beiṫ, to be.
ġan a beiṫ, not to be (without being).
ċum a beiṫ, for the purpose of being.
le beiṫ, in order to be (for to be).
aġ beiṫ, (at being) being.

air beiṫ, air m-beiṫ } on being, having been.
iar m-beiṫ, after being, having been,
air ṫí beiṫ (on the point of being), about to be.

OBS.—beiṫ is the verbal noun *being*, from which are formed the infinitive mood and participles by prefixing certain prepositions.

EXERCISE VIII

carcar, a prison.
cille (*gen.*), of a church
cuir (*past*), put, set (*as seed*).
rearaib (*dat plur.*), men.

meuouiġṫe, increased.
óroiuġ, order.
riol, seed.
rluaġ, a multitude.
caraiḋ, quick.
ġo caraiḋ, quickly.
cionól, an assembly.

INFIN. MOOD, PARTICIPLES, &C.

1. A beiṫ no ɕan a beiṫ. 2. Támaoiṽ iap m-beiṫ aɕ an m-baile mór. 3. Aip m-beiṫ ann a ċoolaṽ ꝺe Ḋómnall.* 4. Iap m-beiṫ ꝺe na peapaiṽ ṽúnca puap a ɕ-capcap. 5. Ḃiṽeaṽap aip cí beiṫ pɕmopca. 6. Aip m-beiṫ ꝺe'n cionól lionca leip an pluaɕ. 7. Ip maiṫ an niṽ a beiṫ úṁal. 8. Ꝺ'óp-ꝺuiɕ pé ꝺoippe na cille beiṫ ṽúnca. 9. Tá an niṽ pin le beiṫ ꝺeunca ɕo capaiṽ. 10. Ꝺo ċuip pé an piol ċum a beiṫ meuꝺuiɕṫe.

* Ann a ċoolaṽ (pron. colla), in his sleep, i. e., asleep.

OBS.—Aip, *on*, in some idiomatic expressions and before verbal nouns causes eclipsis, as in No. 3 above. When a verbal noun follows prepositions, the construction is equivalent to an ablative absolute in Latin, and the verbal noun is generally followed by a preposition governing the dependent noun in the dative, as above.

Additional forms of ꝺo beiṫ.

ɕup aḃ, that it was,\
ꝺap aḃ, to whom was,\
ɕup mé, that it is I,\
an mé, whether (is it) I,\
ní mé, it is not I.

&c. Subjunctive o secondary forms of ip.

ɕo m-buṽ, that it may, &c., optative of ip.

OBS.—Though the forms given above are in grammatical value subjunctive and optative, yet these moods have not a distinct form in Irish.

The moods and tenses apparently wanting are supplied by certain particles, which give a different meaning to the various tenses of the indicative mood, without changing its form except in the verb ꝺo beiṫ and a few irregular verbs.

These particles, as a rule, affect the initials of the verbs they go before. Thus the form of the verb which some grammarians call subjunctive is only, like b-ꝑuiL and ꞃaib for cá and bí, a secondary form of the indicative, to which different shades of meaning are given by the various particles which precede it. This form, as before shown, does not exist in the present tense of iꞅ, but is merely conveyed by the particle and pronoun, the verb being omitted. In the perfect, however, ab may be said to be such a form.

The particle ɼo is used before the affected forms of the verb with a subjunctive meaning, and before buḋ and ꞃaib frequently in an optative sense. When used in sentences in which iꞅ would be the verb employed, it becomes ɼuꞃ, and ab (the secondary form of iꞅ) is omitted; as, ʋeiꞃim ɼuꞃ mé, I say that it is I, for ʋeiꞃim ɼuꞃ ab mé.

ab, a form of buḋ or ba, is the subjunctive of iꞅ, which is employed in certain idiomatic expressions; as, ʋeiꞃim ɼuꞃ ab eaḋ; or contractedly, ʋeiꞃim ɼuꞃ b'eaḋ, I say that it is.

ab is also used in such phrases as ꝼeaꞃ ʋaꞃ ab ainm eoin, i.e., a man to whom is name John—whose name was John. ʋo a ꞃ-ab is the full phrase here; ꞃ is merely euphonic, n is sometimes written in its place, as ʋa n-ab, which would be more easily distinguished from the form in the past tense, ʋaꞃ b' ainm, i.e., ʋo a ꞃo buḋ ainm. In the present tense ꞃ or n is prefixed to ab; in the past tense b for buḋ is aspirated after ꞃo.

So ꝼeaꞃ ʋ'a ɼ-cluinim, i.e. a man of those whom I hear, (*present*); ꝼeaꞃ ʋaꞃ ċualaꞃ, i.e. ꝼeaꞃ ʋo a ꞃo ċualaꞃ, a man of those whom I heard (*past*).

eaḋ is a form of the pronoun é, which is used when a clause of a sentence is the antecedent. eaḋ is also used in such expressions as an eaḋ? is it (forsooth)? iꞅ eaḋ or 'ꞃeaḋ, it is (yes); and ní h-eaḋ, it is not, (no); also in maiꞃeaḋ (for má iꞅ eaḋ, if it is it), if so, well.

When ɼo is used before buḋ, the past tense of iꞅ, it forms as it were the optative mood of that verb; as ɼo m-buḋ me, that I may be. ɼo with ꞃaib has also an optative meaning; as ɼo ꞃaib cú ꞅlán, mayst thou be well.

OBSERVATIONS.

ɼo does not become ɼuṅ for the past tense of ꞃo beiṫ, nor ᴀn, ᴀṅ, nor ní, níoṅ, since in the form of the past tense which would be required after these particles, i.e., ṗᴀib, the ṅo which is incorporated with these is already present. buṫ often aspirates the initial of the word which follows it, as, buṫ ḃpeᴀ́ɼ é, it was fine; buṫ ṁiᴀn liom, it was a wish with me, I wished. When the word following buṫ begins with a vowel or ꞃ followed by a vowel, ꞃo is often prefixed to buṫ and joined with it; as, ꞃob'óɼ í, she was young; ꞃo b'ḟeᴀ́ṅṅ liom, it were better with me, I would prefer, &c.

NOTE.—Any question in which the verb iꞃ is used, or the interrogative particles without a verb, may be answered by the various forms of the verb iꞃ. If ḃ-ꞃuil be the form employed, the answer must be tᴀ́, or ní ḃ-ꞃuil (contractedly ní'l). In the case of other forms of ꞃo beiṫ and in all other verbs it is necessary in answering a question to repeat the verb, and if negative to use the proper particle.

EXERCISE IX.

Examples of the foregoing.

Ciᴀn, Kian, a man's name.
ꞃóiɼ, a supposition.
ꞃeᴀꞃꞃᴀ, henceforth.
Ḟeiṫlim, Felim (Felix)
ɼluᴀꞃᴀċt, to repair, proceed.
X mᴀiꞃeᴀṫ, well.
X ꞃeᴀṫ, yes, it is.

1. ɼo ṗᴀib mᴀiṫ ᴀɼᴀt. 2. Mᴀiꞃeᴀṫ, iꞃ tú ᴀn ꞃeᴀṅ ᴀ tᴀ́ ɼlic. 3. Iꞃ ꞃóiɼ liom ɼuṅ b'eᴀṫ. 4. Tᴀ́ ꞃeᴀṅ ꞃᴀṅ b'ᴀinm Tᴀóɼ ᴀnnꞃ ᴀn ꞃ-tiɼ ṅin ᴀnoiꞃ. 5. Iꞃ ꞃóiɼ liom ɼuṅ mé ᴀn ꞃeᴀṅ ᴀ beiṫeᴀꞃ ᴀnnꞃ ᴀn ɼ-cill. 6. Ⱥn tú ᴀ tᴀ́ ᴀnn? 7. Iꞃ mé ɼo ꞃeiṁin. 8. Ḃ-ꞃuil tú ꞃlᴀ́n? 9. Tᴀ́im, buiṫeᴀċᴀꞃ le

THE VERB do beit.

Ⅾiɑ. 10. buḋ mian liom feaṛɒa ɡluaṛaċċ 11. Ɒob' óɡ aɡuṛ ɒob' áluinn í. 12. Ḃ-ḟuil ɒo máċaiṛ beo fóṛ? 13. Ní'l, tá ṛí maṛḃ, faɒ ó ḟoin. 14. An é ṛo an ḟeaṛ ɒaṛ ab ainm Feiṛlim? 15. Ní h-é, iṛ ṛé Cian a ainm. 16. An laḃṛann tú Ɡaeḋilɡe? 17. Laḃṛaim Ɡaeḋilɡe a tá coṁ miliṛ le mil 18. Ní laḃṛaim ḟóṛ í, aċt táim aɡ ṛóɡluiṛ na ceanɡan ṛin. 19. beata an ṛtáṛaiḋ ṛiṛinne. 20. beata ɒuine a ċoil.

Exercise X.

ain ɒo bí, a time there was.
biḋ, of food, (gen. of biaḋ.)
aɡ iaṛṛaiḋ biḋ, in search of food.
caṛn-aoiliɡ, a dung-heap.
ciall, céill (*dat.*) } sense.
ciallṁaṛ, sensible.
coileaċ, a cock.
cṛóit, shake, flap.
ɒo ċṛóit ṛe a ṛɡiaċáin, he flapped his wings.
ɒoṁan, world.
an ɒoṁan uile, the whole world.
ṛuaiṛ, found.

ɡaṛɒa, spruce.
ɡṛáinne, a grain.
ɡṛáinne ɒ'óṛna, a grain o barley.
iaṛṛaiḋ, searching.
ⅹlóɡṁaṛ, precious.
óṛna, barley.
ṛciataċáin, wings.
(pl. of ṛciataċán.)
ṛɡṛíobaḋ, scratching, scraping.
(from ṛɡṛíob, scrape.)
tábaċt, substance, value.
taṛcuiṛne, contempt.
uiṛṛi, on her, on it

Séoḋ, a jewel.

An Coileać aguſ an Seoð.

Am do bí coileać óg garda aiṗ caṗn-aoiṅ, aiṗ a ṗaib ſé ag ſgṁobað ag iaṗṗaið nð, ſuaiṗ ſé ann cloć lógṁaṗ aiṗ nać ṗaib ioſ aige, cað é an nið é ać go ṗaib ſé io-ðeaſ. Do ćṗóić ſé a ſgiać́ain, aguſ do aḃaiṗ ſé maṗ ſo cṗe ćaṗcuiſne uiṗṗi: "Iſ nið áluinn deaſ ću, go deiṁin, do'n ćé ag a i-ſuil meaſ oṗć, ać do b'ſeáṗṗ liom ſéin .on gṗáinne aṁáin d'óṗna ṁaić, a beić .gam, ioná gać ſeod d'a b-ſuil annſ an ioṁan uile."

Buð ćialĺṁaṗ an coileać é; ać an huinćiṗ ag a b-ſuil ćaṗcuiſne aiṗ nið gið ;uṗ lógṁaṗ é, uaiṗ nać b-ſuil ſioſ aca .iṗ a ćábać, iſ daoine gan céill iad.

Note.—The following paradigm or table of the verb do beić, *to be*, is arranged to suit the Exercises given in this vork. The spelling of various inflections is, as yet rather insettled, and suggestions for its improvement are solicited rom Irish scholars. The views of practical teachers of rish on the spelling of the language and other points u this and the two preceding works of the series will be velcome to the compilers who are anxious that these ext-books should be, in some sort, a standard of modern rish, and free from provincialisms. Some slight changes rom the system laid down by the most generally received uthorities, have been made in order that the Irish Language hall not lose the benefit of modern research and of the abours of our most earnest workers.

TABLE OF THE VERB do beiṫ, to be.

INDICATIVE MOOD.
PRESENT TENSE.

		SINGULAR		PLURAL	
		Synthetic.	Analytic.	Synthetic.	Analytic.
Primary	1.	táim.	tá mé.	támaoid.	tá sinn.
	2.	táir.	— tú.	tátaoi.	— siḃ.
	3.		tá sé, sí.	táid.	— siad.
Secondary	1.	fuilim.	fuil mé.	fuilmíd.	fuil sinn.
	2.	fuilir.	— tú.	fuiltí.	— siḃ.
	3.		fuil sé, sí.	fuilid.	— siad.
Habitual	1.	bíoim.	bíocann mé.	bíoimíd.	bíocann sinn.
	2.	bíoir.	— tú.	bíoċí.	— siḃ.
	3.	bíd or bíocann sé, sí.		bíoid.	— siad.
	—	bím, bír, bíonn sé.		bímís, bíṫí, bíd.	
Assertive	1.		is mé.		is sinn. (inn.)
	2.		is tú. (ṫú.)		is siḃ. (iḃ.)
	3.		is sé, sí. (é, í.)		is siad. (iad.)
		2nd form aḃ, &c.		2nd form aḃ, &c.	

INDICATIVE MOOD.

PAST TENSE.

Primary.
1. bhídheas.   bhí mé.
2. bhíois.   — tú.
3.   bhí ré, rí.
— bíor, bir, bío ré.

	bf mnn.
	— rib.
	— mad.

bíomar, bíobar, bíodar.

Secondary.
1. rabhar.   raib mé.
2. rabhair.   — tú.
3.   raib (or raibhe) ré, rí.

rabhamar.   raib mnn.
rabhabar.   — rib.
rabhadar.   — mad.

Habitual.
1. bhínn.   bhídheadh mé.
2. bhíteá.   — tú.
3.   bhídheadh, ré, rí.
— binn, bíteá, bíodh ré.

bhrómir.   bhídheadh mnn.
bhítí.   — rib.
bíoir.   — mad.
— bímír, bítí, bídír.

Assertive.
1.   budh mé.
2.   budh tú.
3.   budh ré, h-é.

                     budh mnn.
                     budh rib.
                     budh mad, h-iad.

FUTURE TENSE.

1. beidheadh.   beidh mé.
2. beidhir.   — tú.
3.   beidh ré, rí.
— biadh, biair, biaidh ré.
bur, bu, or bidh mé, &c., fut. of ir.

betrómiro.   beidh mnn.
betoití.   — rib.
betoío.   — mad.
— biamaoid, biadaoi, biaid.
beidheas, *relative form.*

TABLE OF THE VERB do beiṫ—Continued.

	SINGULAR.		PLURAL.	
	Synthetic.	Analytic.	Synthetic.	Analytic.
CONDI-TIONAL.	1. beiḋinn 2. beiḋṫeá 3. beiḋeaḋ ré, rí. — beinn, beiṫeá. dá m-baḋ mé, &c. cond. of ir.	beiḋeaḋ mé. — tú.	1. beiḋmír. 2. beiḋṫí. 3. beiḋír. — beimír, &c.	beiḋeaḋ rinn. — ríb. — riad.
IMPERA-TIVE.	1. . . . . 2. bí. 3. bíḋeaḋ ré, rí. — bíoḋ ré, &c.		1. bimír, bímid (bíom). 2. bíoíd. 3. bíoír.	
	INFINITIVE. do or a beiṫ, ġan, ċum, and le beiṫ,		PARTICIPLES. ag beiṫ. air m-beiṫ.	air tí beiṫ. iar m-beiṫ.

PART II.

THE VERB ʋo ḃeiṫ WITH THE PREPOSITIONAL PRONOUNS.

PREPOSITIONS are often compounded with the personal pronouns, so as to form but one word. Many ideas are expressed in a peculiarly idiomatic manner by the words thus formed, in conjunction with the verb ʋo ḃeiṫ. In particular, the idea presented in English by the verb *to have*, is expressed in Irish by the verb ʋo ḃeiṫ, with the aid of the preposition ᴀʒ in its compound form. Thus, possession of a thing is usually expressed in English by saying that the owner has (or had, &c.) the thing; but in Irish by saying that the thing is *at* (or in possession of) the owner. The preposition Le, in the same way, with the assertive verb iꞅ, is used to express ownership in a more absolute sense than ᴀʒ with ᴛá. (See page 47.)

These two idioms shall now be explained. In Section I. of this part will be shown what has been incidentally explained already to some extent, namely, the manner in which these prepositional pronouns, so often met with, are compounded, and how the various forms, in full, of all the prepositions may be employed. In Section II. shall be shown their use with the verb ʋo ḃeiṫ, as denoting possession or ownership.

SECTION I.

THE PREPOSITIONAL PRONOUNS.

The prepositions which unite with the personal pronouns are the following:—

1. ag, at, with.
2. ɑıp, on, upon.
3. ɑnn, in.
4. ɑp, out of.
5. cum, to, towards.
6. ꝺe, of, off, from.
7. ꝺo, to.
8. ıꝺıp, between, among.
9. pá or paoı, under.
10. Le or pe, with.
11. ó or uɑ, from.
12. poıṁ, before.
13. tɑp, beyond, over.
14. tpé, through.
15. um uım or ıom, about.

The personal pronouns are as follows :—

mé, I.
tú, tú, thou, thee.
pé, é, he, him.
pí, í, she, her.

pınn, ınn, we, us.
pıḃ, ıḃ, you, ye.
pıɑꝺ, ıɑꝺ, they.

The second forms shown are, generally speaking, accusative or objective cases of the pronouns, which are also used as nominatives (rather than the primary forms) with the passive voice, and often with the assertive verb ıp. These forms are used when the pronoun is the object of the action; as, ꝺo buɑıL pé é, he struck him.

Certain particles are used after each of these pronouns, which particles have in themselves no apparent special meaning, but give an emphatic force to the pronoun. They can be used also with the pronouns compounded with prepositions, as will be seen, and are often used after nouns and sometimes after verbs. They are as follows.

ꞅa, ꞅan (or ꞅean), ꞅe, ne : thus :—

mıꞅe, or me-ꞅı, I.
ꞅınn-ne, ınn-ne, we, us.
tuꞅa, ṫuꞅa, thou, thee.
ꞅıḃ-ꞅe, ıḃ-ꞅe, you, you.
ꞅé-ꞅean, é-ꞅean, he, him.
ꞅıad-ꞅan, ıad-ꞅan, they, themselves.
ꞅí-ꞅe, í-ꞅe, she, her.

When used after a noun they are joined to it in the same way as mo leaḃaꞃ-ꞅa, my book.

The possessive pronouns are as follow :—

mo, my.
aꞃ, our.
do, thy.
ḃuꞃ, you.
a, his, her.
a, their.

The emphatic particles can be used also with these, but the object must be expressed. We could not say ıꞅ ꞅé mo-ꞅa, *it is mine, &c.* The object must be expressed; as, ıꞅ ꞅé mo leaḃaꞃ-ꞅa é, *it is my book.*

Exercise I.

1. aṡ. 2. aıꞃ. 3. ann.

1. aṡam, at me.
aṡainn, at us.
aṡat, at thee.
aṡaıḃ, at you.
aıṡe, at him.
aca, at them.
aıcı (aıce), at her.

2. oɼm, on me.　　　oɼᴀinn, on us.
　 oɼᴄ, on thee.　　oɼɼᴀib, on you.
　 ᴀiɼ, on him.　　 oɼɼᴀ, on them.
　 uiɼɼi (uiɼɼe), on her.

3. ionnᴀm, in me　　ionnᴀinn, in us.
　 ionnᴀᴄ, in thee　ionnᴀib, in you.
　 ᴀnn, in him.　　 ionnᴄᴀ, in them.
　 innᴄi, (innᴄe), in her.

Obs.—Aɡᴀm, &c., are compounded of aɡ and mé, &c. Oɼm, &c., of ᴀiɼ, and mé, &c.: ᴀɼᴀm, &c., of ᴀɼ and mé, &c. In most of these combinations the pronoun which forms part is easily distinguished; in some, however, it is not so clear; as, ᴀcᴀ from aɡ and ᴀ, a possessive or oblique form of iᴀᴅ, oɼɼᴀ from ᴀiɼ and ᴀ, &c.
The preposition ᴀnn becomes ionn, &c., when compounded.

Exercise II.

4. ᴀɼ.　5. ċum.　6. ᴅe.　7. ᴅo.

4. ᴀɼᴀm, out of me.　　ᴀɼᴀinn, out of us.
　 ᴀɼᴀᴄ, out of thee.　ᴀɼᴀib, out of you.
　 ᴀɼ, out of him.　　 ᴀɼᴄᴀ, out of them.
　 ᴀiɼᴄi (ᴀiɼᴄe), out of her.

5. ċuɡᴀm (towards or)　ċuɡᴀinn, unto us.
　　 unto me.　　　　　ċuɡᴀib, unto you.
　 ċuɡᴀᴄ, unto thee.　 ċucᴀ, unto them.
　 ċuiɡe, unto him.
　 ċuici, unto her.

WITH THE PREP. PRONOUNS 39

6. ᴅíom, off me. ᴅínn, off us.
   ᴅíoc, off thee. ᴅíḃ, off you.
   ᴅé, off him. ᴅíoḃ (or ᴅıu) off them.
   ᴅí, off her.

7. ᴅᴀm, to me. ᴅuınn, to us.
   ᴅuıc, to thee. ᴅᴀoıḃ, to you.
   ᴅó, to him. ᴅóıḃ, to them.
   ᴅí, to her.

Obs.—The preposition ċum becomes when compounded ċuġᴀm, &c., which are pronounced in the South as if written ċuġᴀm, with ġ aspirated. The initial ċ is aspirated, because ċum, which is the root, is in reality a noun, governed by the preposition ᴅo understood. ᴅe and ᴅo are often incorrectly used for each other. Some of these prepositional pronouns, as ᴀıġe, have a special form for the third person masculine. In others, as ᴀr and ᴅé, the preposition itself is employed as an equivalent for the compound form.

Exercise III.

8. ıᴅır. 9. ꜰᴀoı. 10. ʟe. 11. ó.

8. eᴀᴅrᴀm, between me. eᴀᴅrᴀınn, between us
   eᴀᴅrᴀc, between thee. eᴀᴅrᴀıḃ, between you.
   ıᴅır é, ı, between him, her. eᴀᴅᴀrrᴀ, (eᴀcorrᴀ) between them.

9. ꜰúm, under me. ꜰúınn, under us.
   ꜰúc, under thee. ꜰúıḃ, under you.
   ꜰᴀoı, under him. ꜰúcᴀ, under them.
   ꜰúıċı (ꜰúıċe), under her.

THE VERB DO BEIT

10. Liom, Leam, with me. Linn, with us.
    Leac, with thee. Lib, with you.
    Leir, with him. Leo, with them.
    Léi, Léice, with her,
    or piom, pioc, pir, pia : pinn, pib, piú.

11. uaim, from me. uainn, from us.
    uaic, from thee. uaib, from you.
    uaió, from him. uaca, from them.
    uaici, (uaice,) from her.

Toip becomes eavap, and ó ua in composition.
Le and pe are the same. The latter is not now used in the spoken language, but is seen very frequently in books, and always in the Gaelic of Scotland.

Exercise IV.

12. póim. 13. cap. 14. cpé. 15. um.

12. pomam, before me. pomainn, before us.
    pomac, before thee. pomaib, before you.
    pome, before him. pómpa, before them.
    poimpi, before her.

13. capm, over me. capainn, over us.
    capc, over thee. capaib, over you.
    caipip, over him. cáppa, cáppca, over them.
    cáippi, (cáippe,) over her.

14. τρίom, through me.   τρίnn, through us.
    τρίοτ,   through   τρίb, through you.
    thee.
    τρίυ, through him.   τρίοτα, through them.
    τρίčι, through her.

15. umam, about me.   umainn, about us.
    umat, about thee. umaib, about you.
    uime, about him.   umpa, about them.
    uimpi, about her.

Obs.—Combinations with ρεać, beside, as ρεαćam, &c., and with uaρ, over, above, were formerly in use. Those with ρεać are now very seldom met with; those with uaρ never. Instead of uaρam, over me, &c., the phrase όρ mo ćionn, i.e., over (my) head, &c., is now employed.

ταρ becomes ταρm, &c., in composition, the τ being aspirated.

The emphatic suffixes above shown can be used with all the prepositional pronouns, as in the following examples:—

azam-ρα.   αραinn-ne.
ouit-ρe.   oραib-ρe.
leiρ-ρean.   umpa-ραn.
uiρρι-ρe.

Obs.—The particle ρα becomes ρe or ρι when a slender vowel precedes it in the word to which it is affixed. Thus ρα, ρe, and ρι are employed indifferently after the first and second person singular, and the second plural. San (ρean after a slender vowel) is used for the third singular and plural, and ne for the first person plural.

Exercise V.

a nocṡ, to-night.
compare a péip, a n-oé, a n-oiu.
aoinfeaċt, one time.
aon, one and, reaċt, a time, a n-aoinfeaċt le, together with.
bpat, a garment.
coimoeaċt, attendance, protection.
a g-coimoeaċt le, in company with
falluing, a cloak.
falluing ríooa, a cloak of silk.

faitċear, fear.
feaptainn, rain.
ag feaptainn, at rain, raining.
map aon le, together with.
nuaṫ, new.
póg, a kiss.
rit, run.
roc, frost.
ag roc, at freezing.
ríooa, silk (of silk).
rneaċta, snow.
ag rneaċta, snowing.
úo, that, yonder.

A.

1. B-fuil oo leabap agat? 2. Tá mo leabap agur mo peann agam-ra. 3. An m-beiṫ tú map aon liom ag oul go Luimnig? 4. Beiṫeaṫ a g-coimoeaċt leat-ra ag oul go Luimnig a noċt. 5. Cuip oo bairreuo nuaṫ opt. 6. Cuip opt-ra oo bróga. 7. Cuip o'falluing ríooa umat. 8. Tá bpat oearg uime-rean. 9. Labaip leir. 10. Tá rgeul agam ouit.

B.

1. Ná biöeaó faitċeaɼ opt. 2. Cao iɼ ainm ouit—Lopcan no páopaic? 3. Iɼɼé Taöʒ iɼ ainm ɔam. 4. Ɔeun mait ɔóiƀ. 5. Fan ann ɼo, aʒuɼ beiɔeaɔ a n-aoinfeaċt leat-ɼa aiɼ ball. 6. An leat-ɼa an teaċ ɼo? 7. Ní liom-ɼa é aċt iɼ leiɼ an ƀ-feaɼ úɔ é. 8. Ƅeiɔ feaɼtainn aʒainn. 9. Tá ɼé aʒ feaɼtainn. 10. Ní ƀ-fuil ɼé aʒ ɼioc.

C.

1. Tá ceo ann. 2. Ní ƀ-fuil; tá ɼé aʒ ɼneaċta. 3. Ní ƀ-fuil annɼ an t-ɼaoʒal ɼo aċt ceo. 4. Iɼ móɼ an ceo a tá ann. 5. Taƀaiɼ ɔam ɔo lám. 6. Taƀaiɼ ɔam póʒ. 7. Taɼ ċuʒam. 8. Ná ɼit uaim. 9. Tá ɼé aʒ ɔul ċaɼainn. 10. Tá aiɼʒeaɔ aʒuɼ óɼ aʒaiƀ-ɼe.

OBS.—aʒ, is used before the verbal noun (or infinitive mood) to form participles, as above aʒ ɔul (at going). Tá ceo ann &c.—lit, a mist is in it, i.e., there is a mist.

EXERCISE VI.

Some prepositions combine also with the possessive pronouns, but to a very limited extent. The following are the principal instances:—

1. ᴅom', to my.   ᴅ'ɑp, to our.
   ᴅoᴅ', to thy.   ᴅo ƀup, to your.
   ᴅ'ɑ, to his, her.   ᴅ'ɑ, to their.
2. ꞃom', under my.   ꞃo'p, under our.
   ꞃoᴅ', under thy.   ꞃo ƀup, under your.
   ꞃo n-ɑ, under his, her ꞃo n-ɑ, under their.
3. ɑm', in my.   'nɑp, in our.
   ɑᴅ', in thy.   ɑnn ƀup, in your.
   ɑ n-ɑ, or 'nɑ, in his, her.   ɑnn ɑ or 'nɑ, in their.
4. Lem', with my.   Le ɑp, Le'p, with our.
   Leᴅ,' with thy.   Le ƀup, with your.
   Le n-ɑ, with his, her.   Le n-ɑ, with their.
5. óm', from my.   ó ɑp ó'p, from our.
   óᴅ', from thy.   ó ƀup, from your.
   ó n-ɑ, from his, her.   ó n-ɑ, from their.

Obs.—The best authorities recommend that these combinations should, for the sake of clearness, be written as above with hyphens connecting the adventitious letters and with apostrophes to show where a letter or more has been left out. These forms are in frequent use, especially in poetry. The full words are sometimes used, as ᴅo mo instead of ᴅom' *to my*, &c. ɑm' ɑᴅ', &c., are in constant use in a peculiar idiom relating to the use of cá, which verb can never ascribe a predicate to its subject without the use of the preposition ɑ or ɑnn, *in*, as *he is a man* must be rendered, cá ꞃé 'nɑ ꞃeɑp, *he is in his man* (that is, perhaps, in the state of a man). ıꞅ, however, does not require this construction.

Exercise VII.

Mion-ḟoclóıṗ.

aıṗ ḟaḋ, entirely.
caıllṫeaṗ, is lost.
cıṗḋe, a treasure.
an cıṗḋe óıṗ aıṗ ḟaḋ, the entire treasure of gold.
ḋúıl, longing, desire.
eıle, another.
maṗ ᵹaċ ᵹé eıle, as every other goose.
ıomaṗcuıḋ, too much, superfluity.
ıomlán, full, entire.
an t-ıomlán, the whole.

maṗḃ, kill.
ḋo ṁaṗḃ ṗí an ᵹé, she killed the goose.
maṗ ṗın ḋe, as that of it; accordingly.
mıon-ḟoclóıṗ, a vocabulary.
mıon, small, ḟoclóıṗ, a dictionary.
mnaoı (dat. of bean), a woman.
óṗḋa, golden.
ṗuᵹ, bore, laid.
a ṗuᵹ, which laid.

An ᵹé a ṗuᵹ uıḃe óṗḋa.

Ḋo ḃí bean ann, ḟaḋ ó ḟoın, aᵹuṗ ḃí ᵹé aıcı. Ḋo ṗuᵹ an ᵹé ṗo uḃ óṗḋa ᵹaċ maıḋın. Ḃuḋ ṁıan leıṗ an mnaoı an cıṗḋe óıṗ aıṗ ḟaḋ a ḃeıṫ aıcı; aᵹuṗ maṗ ṗın ḋé, ḋo ṁaṗḃ ṗí an ᵹé—aᵹuṗ ḟuaıṗ ṗí naċ ṗaıḃ óṗ aıṗ ḃıṫ annṗ an nᵹé, aᵹuṗ ᵹo ṗaıḃ ṗí maṗ ᵹaċ ᵹé eıle.

Le ḋúıl ann ıomaṗcuıḋ, caıllṫeaṗ ᵹo mınıc an t-ıomlán.

N.B.—ᵹé is both masculine and feminine. It is also spelled ᵹeaḋ.

THE VERB do beiṫ

Exercise VIII.

aip ṗon, for the sake of, for.	goid, steal.
bṗíġ, substance.	do ġoid, *(past)* stole.
gan bṗíġ, valueless.	spéim feola, a piece of meat.
bṗoċaiṗe, a butcher.	nió, a thing.
ċonnaiṗc, saw.	pcáṫ, a shadow.
do ċonnaiṗc ṗé, he saw.	pcáṫa, of a shadow.
copaṁlaċṫ, a likeness.	

An Maḋaḋ aġup an pcáṫ.

Do ġoid maḋaḋ spéim feola ap ṫiġ bpoṫaiṗe, aġup do ḃí ṗé aġ ḋul aip ċláṗ ṫap ṗpuṫ a ḃaile, aġup an feoil aiġe ann a ḃeul, 'nuaip do ċonnaiṗc ṗé a ċopaṁlaċṫ féin ġo poilléip annp an t-ṗpuṫ. buḋ ḋóiġ leip ġuṗ aḃ maḋaḋ eile aġup spéim feola aiġe a ḃí ann, aġup buḋ ṁian leip, an dapa spéim a ḃeiṫ aiġe féin maṗ an ġ-ceudna. Leip pin do léim ṗé aip an pcáṫ, aġup aip ḃall do ċuiṫ an spéim a ḃí aiġe uaiḋ annp an t-ṗpuṫ, aġup maṗ pin do ċaill ṗé an t-iomlán.

An té aġ a m-biḋeann dúil ṗó-ṁóṗ ann nió gan bṗíġ, caillṫeaṗ leip ġo minic nió ṫaiṗḃeaċ aip ṗon pcáṫa.

SECTION II.

USE OF ᴀɢ, Le, AND ó, WITH THE VERB
ᴅo beiṫ.

The presence, use, or simply the possession for the time being is in Gaelic conveyed by means of the verb ᴅo beiṫ, *to be*, in all its moods and tenses in the analytic form (except the assertive verb ıꝛ), together with the use of the prepositional pronouns formed from ᴀɢ, at or with; as, ᴀɢᴀm, ᴀɢᴀᴄ, &c., shown in foregoing pages. When a noun is the possessor the simple forms of these prepositions (i.e. not joined with the pronouns) are employed.

The assertive verb ıꝛ, *it is*, and its various forms as shown above, when used with the compound forms of Le, as, Liom, Leᴀᴄ, &c., denote possession, or a right to anything, as owner.

OBS.—All terms which in Englis' convey the idea of ownership, dominion, control—as mine, thine, his, hers, &c., my own, your own, &c., are translated with Le, as, Le Dıᴀ with God, God's.

Where the verb is used ıꝛ, not ᴄá, is the form with Le.

The want of anything and desire to obtain it is generally expressed by the verb ᴅo beiṫ, and the compound for ns of ó or uᴀ; as. uᴀim, uaıc, &c., as cá an c-aıpɼeaᴅ ɼo uaıó, this money is from him (he wants to get it or has lost it.)

OBS.—There are other idiomatic uses of ɩe, which shall be shown in the third part of this book. Besides the use of 6, referred to above, it has also a simple use, that is, where it merely shows the source or origin of a thing; as, ıɼ uaıc an ɩıcıp ɼo, *this letter is from him;* ıɼ uaıc-ɼe ᴅo cáınıc an ꝼuaım ɓınn *it is from thee came the sweet sound.* (*Mac-Hale's Irish Melodies.*)

The subject of the sentence must come between the verb and the prepositional pronoun, as cá aıpɼeaᴅ aɼam, *money is with me, I have money.* The reason is that the thing possessed (aıpɼeaᴅ) is nominative case to cá, *is* (and so comes after the verb), and not as in the corresponding English sentence, *I have money*, in which the noun is in the objective case. So the form cá aɼam is severed in twain, and the part cá (or ɓ-ꝼuıɩ) takes its place first, next the thing or subject (as aıpɼeaᴅ), and lastly, the prepositional pronoun (as aɼam.)

NOTE.—This order of the words holds good, no matter how many subjects to the verb are introduced. They are all, in Irish, nominatives to cá, and, in English, objectives after "have."

EXERCISE I.

It is not necessary to repeat the various forms of ᴅo ɓeıc. One example, therefore, of each shall be given, using ɼé or é, *it*, to

WITH THE PREP. PRONOUNS.

represent the object of the sentence, or the thing which one has, owns, or wants, according to the idiom.

Examples.

Tá ré agam.	I have it.
An b-fuil ré agat?	Hast thou it?
Ní b-fuil ré ag Eoin.	John has not it.
Bídeann ré againn.	We usually have it.
Bí ré agaib.	Ye had it.
An raib ré aca?	Had they it?
Ní raib ré agam-ra.	I had not it (myself).
Bídead ré aige.	He used have it.
Beid ré aici.	She will have it.
Beidead ré agaib.	You would have it.
Bídead ré aca.	Let them have it.
Do beit ag—	To beat (be long to—)
Ag beit ag—	Belonging to—
Is liom-ra é.	I own it.
Bud leir é.	He owned it.
Tá ré uaim.	It is wanting to me.
B-fuil ré uait?	Dost thou want it?

Exercise II.

cáirde, friends
  (*pl.* of cara).
glóir, glory.
glóir do Dia, Glory (be) to

sról, satin.
táinte, flocks
  (*pl.* of táin, a herd, spoil).
uaine, green.

THE VERB do beit

1. Tá airgead agus ór agam. 2. An b-fuil
ríoda agus ról agat? 3. Tá ról uaine
aici. 4. Beid airgead agus ór agus talam
againn. 5. B-fuil airgead agus ór, teac
agus talam—cáipde agus táinte aca? 6.
B-fuil ppné agus talam aici? 7. Tá ppné
talam agus ba aici. 8. Tá mac óg agus
ingean deas ag an b-fear sopa, 9. Tá
papán lán agus maoin mór aige. 10. Tá
lá fada againn, agus tá airgead agus ór
talam agus táinte againn—glóir do Dia.

Exercise III.

Lán, abundance, the full, plenty.

1. Tá cú agam acht ní liom féin é. 2. Tá
airgead agus ór againn acht ní linn iad.
3. Raib mil agus min ag Murcad, agus ar
leir féin iad? 4. Do bí mil agus min aige
agus bud leir féin iad. 5. An m-beid im úr,
agus mil agat? 6. Beid im úr, agus mil
agus arán agam, acht ní bur liom féin
iad, acht le Murcad. 7. An leat-sa an
mac óg, agus an teac mór, agus an capall
láidir? 8. Deir tú gur liom iad: ir liom
an teac mór rin, agus gac nid a tá agam.
9. Ir mór an lán a tá agat. 10. Ir mait
an nid go b-fuil fiad agam, agus gur liom
féin iad

Exercise IV.

bean an tiġe, woman of the house—the goodwife.

cá h-áit, what place, where.

Concubaṗ, Connor.

ꞅeaꞃ an tiġe, man of the house,
i.e., a special house.

ꞅeaꞃ tiġe, a householder.

Fionnġuala, Finola, a woman's name, i.e., ꞅionn ġuala, fair shoulder.

1. Caḋ tá uait? no caḋ tá tú aġ iaꞃꞃaiḋ? 2. Tá mo ḃaiꞃeuḋ uaim-ꞃe; an ḃ-ꞅuil ꞃé aġat-ꞃa? 3. Ní ḃ-ꞅuil ꞃé aġam, aġuꞃ ní ḃ-ꞅuil ꞃoꞃ aġam ca h-áit a ḃ-ꞅuil ꞃé. 4. Tá aiꞃġeaḋ aġam aċt ní liom ꞅéin é. 5. Cia ₋eiꞃ é? 6. Iꞃ lem' ataiꞃ é. 7. Cia leiꞃ an ₋eanḃ óġ ꞃin aġuꞃ caḋ iꞃ ainm ḋó? 8. Iꞃ le ꞅeaꞃ an tiġe é aġuꞃ Concubaꞃ iꞃ ainm ḋó. 9. Iꞃ le bean an tiġe an inġean óġ óeaꞃ ꞃin aġuꞃ Fionnġuala iꞃ ainm ḋi. 10. Ḋá m-baḋ léi an bean óġ úḋ maꞃ inġean baḋ ꞃona an bean í.

Obs.—In the foregoing exercises the use of tá with aġ ınd iꞃ with le is contrasted. A careful study of these exei-:ises will render these idioms more familiar to the learner han any explanation could.

Exercise V.

1. Céaḋ mile ꞅáilte ꞃómat. 2. Tá naoi ġ-céaḋ mile ꞅáilte aġam-ꞃa ꞃómat. 3. Iꞃ onṁuin tú lem' ċꞃoiḋe. 4. Tá caꞃa nait ꞃioꞃ aꞅam. 5. Tá ꞃé 'na caꞃa

THE VERB DO ḃeiṫ

maiṫ ɼeaɼṁaċ ḋam, aᵹuɼ iɼ aiᵹe-ɼean a ṫá maoin ṁóɼ. 6. Iɼ liḃ-ɼe an ɼaiöḃɼeaɼ. 7. Iɼ Leo-ɼan aᵹuɼ leḋ' aṫaiɼ é. 8. Iɼ móɼ an ṁaoin a ṫá aᵹaṫ-ɼa. 9. Ḃ-ɼuil lea- ḃaɼ Ꝼaeḋilᵹe aiɼ biṫ aᵹaṫ-ɼa? 10. Ṫá an ċeuḋ leaḃaɼ aᵹuɼ an ḋaɼa leaḃaɼ aᵹam aᵹuɼ iɼ liom ɼéin iaḋ.

NOTE.—It is a peculiarity in Gaelic that the substantive verb ṫá can never ascribe a nominal predicate, *i.e.*, a predicate which is a noun, to its subject, without the aid of the preposition 1 or ann, *in.*—See No. 5 above.
Iɼ, as before shown, does not require this use of ann.

EXERCISE VI.

caoiɼiᵹ, sheep.
(*pl.* of caoɼa.)
cóiɼ, right.

iɼ cóiɼ ḋuiṫ, it is right for thee, i.e., you ought.
uain, lambs.

1. Ḃuḋ liom-ɼa an ṫeaċ ɼin. 2. Aɼ leaṫ- ɼa an capall aᵹuɼ na caoiɼiᵹ? 3. Iɼ le mo ḋeaɼḃ ɼṫaiɼ iaḋ-ɼan. 4. Iɼ cóiɼ ḋuiṫ, capall a ḃeiṫ aᵹaṫ, ḋuiṫ ɼéin. 5. Ṫá mé ann ɼo boċṫ, ḋona, ᵹan capall no aɼal a ḃeiṫ aᵹam-ɼa ḋam ɼéin. 6. Ḃeiḋ capall aᵹaṫ aiɼ ball, aᵹuɼ ṫeaċ, ṫalaṁ aᵹuɼ ṫáinṫe, uain aᵹuɼ caoiɼiᵹ; aᵹuɼ iaḋ uile ḋoḋ' ċuiḋ ɼéin. 7. Ṫáim liom ɼéin anoiɼ. 8. Ḋo ḃiḋiɼ leaṫ ɼéin an ṫ-am ɼin. 9. Ḃeiḋ ɼí léi ɼéin annɼ an ṫiᵹ. 10. Ṫámaoiḋ linn ɼéin aiɼ an ṫ-ɼaoᵹal.

OBS.—An idiomatic yet familiar use of le (with ṫá, not iɼ in this case) is shown in the last four sentences of the preceding exercise. Here liom ɼéin, *with or by myself*, signifies *alone*.

WITH THE PREP. PRONOUNS.

Exercise VII.

ᴀice, near,
  (of place) 'na ᴀice, near him (in his neighbourhood).

bruać, brink.

cloićin, a pebble,
  a small stone; carn cloićín, a pile of pebbles.

deoiż } (*obs.*), end,
diaiż
  only used in phrases like a n-diaiż, behind, diaiż a n-diaiż, after each other. ꝼá deoiż, in fine, &c.

dortad, spilling, to spill.
  an ćruircín do dortad, to spill the pitcher.

eitill, fly.
  d'eitill ré, he flew.

ꝼada, long.
  com ꝼada ríor, so far down. Com ꝼada ríor, so long (a time) down.

ꝼéidir, possible.
  naċar ꝼéidir leir, that it was not possible with him, that he could not.

ꝼíor-uirże, springwater

żáirdeaċar, gladness.

iarraċt, an effort, an attempt.
  do ċuż ré iarraċt, he made an attempt.

muineíl, of a neck.
  muineíl (*gen.* of muineul). Le ríneaḋ a muineíl, with stretching (of) his neck.

preaċán, a crow.

ráruiż, satisfy.
  do ráruiż ré a ċart, he satisfied his thirst.

ríneaḋ, stretching,
  (from rin, stretch.)

teaċt, to come.
  teaċt ċuiże, to come to it.

ċuż, gave, (made.)

An Preaċán agur an Ċruircín.

Air m-beiṫ do preaċán leaṫ-marḃ leir an d-tart, do ċonnairc ré 'na ᴀice cruircín lan d' ꝼíor-uirże. D'eitill ré żo tarai̇ḋ ċ

ngáipveacap móp, agup go cinnte, fuaip fé uipge innte, act vo bí fé com fava fíop annp an g-cpúipcin, nacap féivip leip teact cuige le píneav a muinéil. Do tug fé ippact aip an g-cpúipcin vo vopta, act ní paib neapc go leop ann. Fá veoig, vo connaipc fé capn cloicín a b-fogup, agup vo cuip fé iav viaig a n-viaig annp an g-cpúipcin, agup leip pin vo bí an t-uipge ag bpuac na cpúipcin agup vo fápuig fé a tapt.
Thó a tá vóiveunta le neapc tá fé fói-veunta le ptuaim.

Obs.—The learner will remember that go placed before any adjective gives it the force of an adverb; as above in go tapa, *quickly*, &c.

Cpúipcin is sometimes masculine.

PART III.

IDIOMS.

In this part the idioms in most general use shall be treated of. In the First Section the various idioms in connection with the verb vo beit, which are very expressive, and without some knowledge of which the learner can make but little progress, will be explained— and by careful study of this section, and the former parts of this book, the verb vo beit, which plays so important a part in Gaelic, will

IDIOMS. 55

be quite familiar in all its forms to the learner. In Section II. the idioms in connection with the position of the Adjective, the Nominative case, and Verb, the Genitive case, the Demonstrative pronoun, &c., shall be dealt with.

SECTION I.

IDIOMS OF ᴅo ḃeiṫ.

1. The verb ᴅo ḃeiṫ, with the preposition ᴀiɼ, *on*, gives rise to several idiomatic forms of expression.

All the conditions of the body, the state of the feelings, of the soul, of the mind, are in Gaelic said to be *on* a person (ᴅo ḃeiṫ ᴀiɼ) ; as the primary and secondary qualities, namely, form, figure, length, width, colour, heat, cold, and all the *modal changes* and affections might be said to be *on* the subject in which they reside.

As colour is on the matter coloured, so, in Gaelic, one supposes that passion, anger, hate, love, and the like, are *on* the soul. These traits are modifications, so to say, of the soul; others, like sickness, health, cold, heat, &c., are *on* the body.

Hence, a Gaelic speaker addresses his neighbour not by saying, as in English, *are you cold?* or as in French, *have you cold?* but in this wise, *is cold on thee? is anger on thee?* &c.

56 THE VERB do beiṫ.

Exercise I.
Examples.

Tá ocras orm. (Hunger is on me.) I am hungry
B-fuil fuacṫ ort? (Is cold on thee?) Art thou cold?
Tá tart air. (Thirst is on him.) He is thirsty
Tá tinneas orm. (Sickness is on me). I am sick.
B-fuil eagla oraib. (Is fear on you? *pl.*) Are you afraid?
Tá doilġíos croiḋe orm. (Sorrow of heart is on me.) I am heartily sorry.
Tá brón agus briseaḋ croiḋe[1] air na daoiniḃ Sorrow and breaking of heart are on the people.
Tá fearg air an b-fear sin. (Anger is on that man.) That man is angry.

Exercise II.

The following sentences show this idiom in relation to A, External form; B, Subject matter; C, The feeling; D, Good or bad fortune:—

A.

B-fuil cuma ort. Is there form (or shape) on thee?
Ní b-fuil cuma air biṫ orm. There is no trim *at all* on me (I am not in trim.)

[1] As the vowel i preceding ḋ or ġ (*dotted*) is almost invariably long it is scarcely necessary to mark it with the accent.

IDIOMS.

Feuċ an ċuma¹ a tá ort! See the form which is on thee. (See what a state you are in!)
An é sin an ċuma a tá air do ṁac? Is that the plight that is on thy son? (that your son is in).
b-fuil gné air? Is there any (perceptible) form on it?
Raib daṫ air an euḋaċ? Was there colour on the cloth?

B.

b-fuil slaċt² air bit uirri? Is there any decent appearance (slaċt) on her?
Tá slaċt mór uirri. There is a very good appearance on her. (She is well favoured).
Feuċ an t-euḋan a tá air an b-fear! See the face that is on the man!

C.

Tá gráḋ agam ort-sa. I have love for thee.
Tá cion mór aige-sean ort. He has great regard for thee.
Ní b-fuil meas air an b-fáiḋ, ann a ṫír féin. There is no esteem for (on) the prophet in his own country.

¹ Cuma, as above, is used in reference to one who is, or is not in proper trim in dress or in mind.
² From slaċt is formed the adjective slaċtṁar, well-looking, in good case.

Ní b-ḟuil gráḋ agam air aon neaċ aċt air
Dia aṁáin. I have no love for (on) any·
one, but for God alone.

D.

Tá an t-áḋ orm. (The) luck is on me.
Go raib an t-áḋ agus an t-aṁantur ort.
May luck and happy chance be on thee.
Bail ó Dia ort. Prosperity from God on
thee[1].
Raċ, go raib ort. Prosperity,[2] may (it) be
on thee.
Go g-cuirró Dia an raċ ort. May God put
prosperity on thee.
B-ḟuil bireaċ ort? Is there improvement[3] on
thee?
Tá bireaċ mór orm. There is great improve-
ment on me.
B-ḟuil tinneas air do ṁáṫair? Is there sick-
ness on thy mother.

---

[1] The usual salute of the Irish peasant to one at work.
bail, also success; bailiġ, amass, collect.
[2] Raċ means a (new) state or lot, condition, also advan·
tage, increase; deaġraċ, good luck; droċraċ, bad luck.
[3] Said to one in sickness or in a backward state.

Exercise III.

átaſ, gladness, joy.
ſonn, delight, pleasure.
galaſ, disease.
óiſ, for.
teaſ, heat.

1. An b-ſuil ſuaċt oſt? 2. Tá ſuaċt oſm, aguſ bí ſuaċt oſm; aguſ tá eaglа oſm go m-beið ſuaċt oſm. 3. Raib tinneaſ oſaib? 4. Bí; aguſ tá átaſ oſm naċ b-ſuil ſé anoiſ oſainn. 5. An m-beið taſt oſt? 6. Ní beið taſt oſm, óiſ tá biſeaċ móſ oſm. 7. Ní b-ſuil teaſ no ſuaċt, tinneaſ no galaſ aiſ bit oſm,—buiðeaċaſ le Dia. 8. Ní biðeann bſón no eagla aiſ ſeaſ maiṫ. 9. Go raib ſonaſ aguſ ſeun, aguſ áð aguſ amantuſ oſt. 10. Tá ſonn oſm a beit ag caint leat.

Exercise IV.

The two idioms of the verb ꝺo beiṫ, with agam and aiſ, are often found in the same phrase:

cáil, repute, quality, notice of the people.
ꝺaoineaᵭ (*gen. pl.*) of ꝺuine), of people.
ꝺeo, or ꝺeoig (*obs.*) end; go ꝺeo, for ever.
ſeuċ, see, try.
geаn, affection.
móſán, much, many, a great deal; (governs genitive). móſán ꝺaoineaᵭ, many people.

1. B-ḟuil meaṛ móṗ aġac opm? 2. Tá; aġuṛ cá meaṛ aġam aiṗ ḟeaṛ maic. 3. B-ḟuil ġean aġuṛ ġṗáḋ aġac aiṗ Dia? 4. Tá; aġuṛ bí—aġuṛ beiḋ ġean aġuṛ ġṗáḋ aġam ġo ḋeo aiṗ, óiṗ iṛ ṛé m'acaiṗ é. 5. Tá ġṗáḋ aġam aiṗ Dia, aġuṛ cá ġṗáḋ aġ Dia opm. 6. Feuċ—b-ḟuil cáil aġuṛ meaṛ móṗ opc-ṛa? 7. Tá; cá cáil móṗ opm ann ġaċ áic, aġuṛ cá meaṛ aġ móṗán ḋaoineaḋ opm. 8. Bí ġṗáḋ móṗ aġ m'acaiṗ aġuṛ aġ mo ṁácaiṗ opm, aġuṛ cá ġean aġuṛ ġṗáḋ aġam aiṗ m'acaiṗ aġuṛ aiṗ mo ṁácaiṗ. 9. Tá ṛúil aġam naċ b-ḟuil cinneaṛ, no ġalaṗ, no bṗón, no bṗiṛeaḋ cṗoiḋe opc. 10. Ní b-ḟuil; buiḋeaċaṛ le Dia : ṗlán leac.

Obs.—The learner is now aware that (1) the different states and conditions of the human body; (2) the affections of the soul, and the perceptions and passions of animal life, are declared to be *upon* the person who is the subject of them. One does not say he *has* these sensations, but that they are *on* him. Therefore English sentences of this nature must be translated into Irish, not word for word, but according to idiom.

This special idiom in Gaelic expresses a truth, namely, that colour and the changes of matter rest, as it were, on the substance, and similarly the various affections of the mind or the soul are something that comes over it.

When one receives affection, respect, or favour, or the contrary, he is said to " suffer " from the action of him who bestows such favours,—and the verb expressing such state is in the *passive* voice. In Gaelic this action may be expressed by the verb do beit and the preposition air, as above, and sometimes by the use of the passive voice of verbs.

Exercise V.

Examples of English and Irish idiom.

English.	Literal.	Irish.
What ails thee?	(What is it that is on thee?)	Cad é a tá ort?
I am sick.	(Sickness is on me.)	Tá tinneas orm.
Was your father sick?	Was there sickness on your father?	Raib tinneas air d'ataip?
He is better.	(Improvement is on him.)	Tá bireaċ air. Fuair ré bireaċ.
Art thou afraid?	(Is fear on thee?)	b-fuil eagla ort?
We are very glad that Torloch O'Brien has come safe home.	Big gladness is on us, because Torloch O'Brien is home safe.	Tá luitġáir mór orainn air fat go b-fuil Toirdealbaċ O'briain ṗlán a baile.
I am greatly esteemed.	(There is great esteem on me.)	Tá meas mór orm.
He is beloved.	(Affection is on him.)	Tá ġean air.
They are disliked.	(Dislike is on them.)	Tá ġráin orra.
They are hated.	(Hate is on them.)	Tá fuat orra.

Exercise VI.

Some states of the body and mind are expressed by the adjective and the verb do beit, as well as by the use of the preposition air with that verb

THE VERB do beit.

We say "some states," for all states are not capable of being expressed by the verb and the adjective, and especially where the feeling of one person towards another is intended to be described; as, cá meap opm, I am esteemed (*by others*) is not cá mé meapamail (*I am estimable*); or cá mé meapuigče (*I am valued*.)

NOTE.—The phrase "I am sick," can be expressed by cá mé cinn, *I am sick*, as well as by cá cinneap opm, *sickness is on me*. The difference is that one, cá mé cinn, expresses a special feeling for the moment; the other, cá cinneap opm, a state of sickness which *is on me*. These niceties of the language must be learned by experience.

a meapg, amongst.
a is a preposition and meapg a noun; (i.e., *in midst*), so the phrase requires a genitive case after it.

báid, natural childish love.

blapoa, sweet-sounding.

cion, regard, appreciation, respect, looking up to.

clainn, ⎫ (*dat.*),
clann, ⎬ clan.
        ⎭ children,

daoineaö ⎫ (*gen.*)
daoinib, ⎬ (*dat.*),
          ⎭ people.

(Plural forms of duine.)

deipim, I say.

deipim leac, I say to you.

opoć-meap, disrespect.

gean, affection (of the heart).

gpáin, dislike.

máťapda, maternal.

neać, a person, anyone.

paob, false, erring.

paob-gpád, foolish love.

silly, misplaced love, love for pets.

peapc, fondness, gallantry, wooing.

peapc-gpád, fond love.

love of love; love of mothers for children.

IDIOMS. 63

1. An b-fuil meaṙ móṗ oṗc annṗ an o-ċíṗ ṗo? 2. Tá; aguṗ tá gean aguṗ gṗáḋ ag na ḋaoiniḃ oṗm. 3. Ṙaiḃ gṗáḋ móṗ aiṗ ḋo ṁac, aguṗ aiṗ ḋo ċlainn a meaṗg na n-ḋaoineaḋ? 4. Ḃí; ḋeiṗim leat go ṗaiḃ meaṗ móṗ oṗainn, aguṗ go m-beiḋ cion oṗainn, aċt ní ṗaiḃ aguṗ ní ḃ-fuil go fóil, meaṗ aiṗ aṗ o-teangain ṁín, ṁiliṗ, ṁátaṗ-ḋa. 5. Iṗ olc an níḋ é oṗoċ-ṁeaṗ a ḃeit aiṗ níḋ a tá binn blaṗḋa. 6. Tá ciall agat. 7. Má tá ciall agam, ní ḃ-fuil an ċáil ṗin amuiġ oṗm. 8. Ṙaiḃ cionn aguṗ gean agat oṗc féin? 9. Tá cion aguṗ gean ag gaċ ḋuine aiṗ féin, ṗeaṗc aguṗ gṗáḋ ḋo Ḋia aguṗ ḋ'aṗ muinciṗ. 10. Tá cáil móṗ oṗc; tá meaṗ oṗc; ní ḃ-fuil gṗáin ag aon neaċ oṗc.

OBS.—From the idea of the qualities of a thing resting on the substance, another kindred view is common among Gaelic speakers, namely, that oneself is placed " on " something, as " on board," " on surface," nay, " on " an abstract state or quality—as " on madness," aiṗ buile; in a frolic aiṗ miṗe; drunk, aiṗ meiṗge, &c. See aiṗ ball, aiṗ bit.

NOTE.—If the phrases with aiṗ, *on*, are used in an adverbial sense, and with a wide meaning, the initial consonant of the noun is not aspirated after aiṗ; as, aiṗ báṗṗ, on top.

EXERCISE VII.

The initials of nouns following the preposition ᴀɪɼ are not aspirated when the words are used indefinitely and adverbially; but when specially employed with reference to a certain object, aspiration then takes place as usual.

Thus, aspiration takes place if a special meaning is implied; as, ᴀɪɼ ḃáɼɼ na h-ᴀɪLLe, on the summit of the cliff. ᴀɪɼ in such adverbial phrases sometimes eclipses; as, in ᴀɪɼ ᴠ-ᴛúꞃ in the beginning.

Examples.

1. Ꭺɪɼ maɪᴠɪn, in the morning; ᴀɪɼ ṁaɪᴠɪn ḃɼeág áLuɪnn, on a beautiful fine morning.
2. Ꭺɪɼ meaóon-oɪóce, at midnight. }
   A meaóon-Lae, in mid-day. }
3. Ꭺɪɼ baoɪꞃ (on folly) silly.
4. Ꭺɪɼ bóɼᴠ, on board, on the table; ᴀɪɼ bóɼa Loɪnꞅe, on board a ship.
5. Ꭺɪɼ báɼɼ, on top, superior; ᴀɪɼ ḃáɼɼ na h-ᴀɪLLe, on the top of the cliff.
6. Ꭺɪɼ ꞅ-cúL, in the rear, backward, privately; cuɪɼ ᴀɪɼ ꞅ-cúL, abolish.
7. Ꭺɪɼ aꞅaɪó (*on face*) in front, ahead.
8. Ꭺɪɼ buɪLe, on fury, raging mad.
9. Ꭺɪɼ uaccaɼ, on the surface.
10. Ꭺɪɼ Láɼ, in the middle; Láɼ, level, laid low.

IDIOMS.

11. Aiṗ ṗán, going astray; ṗán, means wandering, not knowing where one is.
12. Aiṗ ṗeaċṗán, wandering apart and out of the path; ṗeaċ, apart.
13. Aiṗ meaṗbaL, raving, wandering in mind.
14. Aiṗ bun, on foundation, established (as an institution); aiṗ bun a ċoiṗe, on the sole of his foot.
15. Aiṗ miṗe, on madness, in a mad state.
16. Aiṗ meiṗge, on drunkenness, drunk.
17. Aiṗ oLcaṗ, in badness, as bad as can be.
18. Aiṗ ṗeabaṗ, in excellence, in first-class style.
19. Aiṗ ṿ-ċúṗ, in the beginning, at first.
20. Aiṗ ṿeiṗe, on end, at the end.

EXERCISE VIII.

aiLLe, of a cliff.
  (*gen.* of aiLL.)
bóṗṿ, a table, a board.
cuan, a harbour, a coast.
  oṗ cionn an ċuain, overhead (of) the coast.
ṿeoṗaċ, tearful.
ṿuL (ag ṿuL), going.
Leun, affliction.
  mo Leun! my sorrow!

Loinge, of a ship.
  (*gen.* of Long.)
óL, drink.
  ag óL, drinking.
oṗ cionn, overhead, above.
ṗeubaṿ (ag ṗeubaṿ), tearing.
ṗeaL, a while.

THE VERB do beiṫ.

1. Dómnall aip meirge agup a bean ag ól uirge. 2. Seal aip meirge, real aip buile; peubaḋ teud a'r dul aip mipe. 3. Aip maidin a n-dé, ir deoraċ do biḋeap-pa. 4. Aip bárr na h-aille or cionn an ċuain. 5. Mo leun! naċ aip bórd loinge tá mé; ann pin, beiḋinn aip reabap. 6. Aip olcap no aip reabap, tá mé map tá mé. 7. Tá ré aip pán agur aip reaċpán. 8. Do ċuip ré iad aip bórd. 9. Ir reápp beiṫ dul aip agaiḋ ioná dul aip g-cúl. 10. Ir reápp coigilt aip d-túr ioná aip deipe. 11. A ṗeanóip a tá aip baoir. 12. Aip maidin a n-dé, poiṁ gréin go moċ.

Obs.—dul aip agaiḋ, going forward, *lit.*, going on face; dul aip g-cúl, going backward, i.e., going on back. Teiḋ aip d'agaiḋ, go ahead, *lit.*, go on your face, &c.

EXERCISE IX.

The following sentences contain words used in the foregoing examples and exercises, and will afford useful additional examples of the forms of do beiṫ, and idioms.

Criortaiḋ, a Christian
geallta, promised.
Led' ṫoil, with thy will or permission.
'nuaip, when.
i.e. an uaip, the time.
órduig, ordain.
d'órduig ré, he ordained.
ríġeaċt, a kingdom.

1 B-ruil gráḋ agat aip Dia? 2. Tá: agur ma tá gráḋ agat-pa aip Dia, tá gráḋ

IDIOMS.

ag Dia opc-ṗa. 3. Tá ꝟean aꝟam, bí ꝟeaꝟ aꝟam aꝟuṗ beiḋ ꝟean aꝟam ꝟo ḋeo aip Dia 4. Iṗ maiṫ an ṗꝟeul é ṗin ó beul an té aꝟ a b-ṗuil ṗioṗ aip anam, an ḋuine, ꝟo b-ṗuil ṗé le beiṫ beo a ṗiꝟeaċt Dé ꝟo ḋeo. 5. An ṗáiḋ tú? 6. Ní ṗáiḋ mé, aċt iṗ Cṗioṗ- taiḋ mé. 7. Anoiṗ, an b-ṗuil ꝟean aꝟuṗ ꝟṗáḋ aꝟat aip ḋ'aṫaiṗ aꝟuṗ aip ḋo ṁáṫaip? 8. Tá; óip ní'l ꝟṗáḋ aꝟ ḋuine aip Dia, 'nuaiṗ naċ b-ṗuil ꝟṗáḋ aiꝟe aip a aṫaip aꝟuṗ aip a ṁáṫaip ṗéin. 9. D'óiṗḋuiꝟ Dia ḋo'n ḋuine ꝟean aꝟuṗ ꝟṗáḋ a beiṫ aiꝟe aip a aṫaip aꝟuṗ aip a ṁáṫaip, aꝟuṗ tá beaṫa ṗaḋa aꝟuṗ ṗeun ꝟeallta ḋo'n té aꝟ a b-ṗuil ꝟṗáḋ aip a aṫaip aꝟuṗ aip a ṁáṫaip ṗéin. 10. Tá tú ceaṗt: tá ꝟean aꝟ ꝟaċ aon aip an té tuꝟ túṗ beaṫa ḋó. 11. B-ṗuil ꝟean aꝟat-ṗa oipt ṗéin? 12. Tá ꝟean aꝟuṗ ṗeaṗc aꝟam aip Dia, aip ḋ-túṗ, aip mo ċip annṗ an ḋaṗa h-áit, opm ṗéin, opt-ṗa, leḋ' ṫoil aꝟuṗ aip ꝟaċ ḋeaꝟ-ḋuine. 13. Tá ḋo ṗait aꝟat ann ṗin. 14. Iṗ áil liom, ꝟean a beiṫ aꝟ ꝟaċ ḋeaꝟ-ḋuine opm-ṗa. 15. Iṗ mian liom ḋo ꝟean a beiṫ opm.

IDIOMS RELATING TO PRICE AND DEBT

There are two other very important idioms in connection with the use of the preposition

ꙅiꞃ with the verb ꞇo ḃeiꞇ. The words ciᴀ
ṁeuꞇ? *how much?* literally, what quantity, size
or amount, are applied either to things foɼ
sale, or to man. If to things for sale, ciᴀ
ṁeuꞇ refers to price or value; if to man, then
these words refer to debt owed by him, as :—

EXERCISE X.

First Instance.—Price.

Ciᴀ ṁeuꞇ ᴀ ꞇá ꙅiꞃ buᴀiḃ.? — How much is on (or for) cows? i.e., What is the price of cows?

Ciᴀ ṁeuꞇ ᴀ ꞇá ꞇú ꞇ' iᴀꞃꞃᴀiꞅ ꙅiꞃ nᴀ cᴀpᴀllᴀiḃ? — How much are you asking for the horses?

Ciᴀ ṁeuꞇ ᴀ ꞇá ꙅiꞃ im? — What is the price of butter?

Ciᴀ meuꞇ ᴀ ꞇá ꙅiꞃ iᴀꞃꞃ ᴀn ceᴀnn? — How much is on fish the head (each per head?)

Ciᴀ ṁeuꞇ ᴀ ꞇá— — *What is the price—*

ꙅiꞃ ḃᴀinne, on milk.
ꙅiꞃ ᴀꞃán, on bread.
ꙅiꞃ coiꞃce, on oats.
ꙅiꞃ óꞃnᴀ, on barley.
ꙅiꞃ ᴀꞃḃᴀꞃ, on corn.
ꙅiꞃ ꝼeoil, on meat.
ꙅiꞃ ꝼion, on wine.
ꙅiꞃ cꞃuiꞇneᴀċꞇ, cn wheat.

ꙅiꞃ coċᴀn, on straw.
ꙅiꞃ ꞅꞃól, on satin.
ꙅiꞃ ꞅioꞇᴀ, on silk.
ꙅiꞃ lineuꞇᴀċ, on linen.
ꙅiꞃ cᴀꞇáꞅ, on cotton.
ꙅiꞃ euꞇᴀċ-cᴀꞇáiꞅ, on calico (cloth of cotton.)

IDIOMS.

N. B.—Cá is used in Munster for ciá, and méid for meud.

OBS.—bá and capaill are nominatives plural; buáib and capallaib datives plural. In this case after a preposition the dative would be required, i.e., buáib and capallaib; but the termination of the dative in ib is now very seldom heard, especially in phrases of this nature.

EXERCISE XI.

aonac, a fair.
caoiriġ, *nom. pl.*
caorcaib, *dat. pl.* sheep.

siúcra, sugar.
tae, tea.

1. Raib tú ag an aonac a n-diu? 2. Bideár. 3. Cad tá air an g-ceann de na capallaib? 4. Bí luac mór air capallaib, agur air buáib, act bí caoiriġ raor go leor. 5. An raib coirce agur cruitneact agur órna raor ann rin? 6. Bí arbar daor act do bí im raor. 7. Cia meud a tá air tae agur air siúcra annr an m-baile mór? 8. Tá rad raor; agur ir mait an rgeul nac b-fuil luac ró-mór anoir orra. 9. An b-fuil luac mór ann rúd anoir air riodá no air rról. 10. Tá rad-ran daor: act ir beag an luac a tá air eudac-cadáir.

EXERCISE XII.

Second Instance.—Debt.

Cia meuḋ a tá ort?	How much is on thee? (How much do you owe?)
Tá fiċe púnt orm.	There are twenty pounds on me. (I owe twenty pounds.)
B-fuil mórán air?	Is there much on him? (Does he owe much?)
Tá caoġaḋ púnt aige orm.	He has fifty pounds on me. (I owe him fifty pounds.)

Caoimġin, Kevin. ċeannuiġeas, I bought.
Caoimġin O'Tuaċail, Kevin O'Tual.

1. B-fuil mórán air d'aṫair? 2. Tá ḋá ċéaḋ púnt air m'aṫair agus tá trí ċéaḋ púnt orm féin. 3. Do ċeannuiġeas capall ag an aonaċ a n-ḋé; buḋ sé a luaċ caoġaḋ púnt; ṫug me ḋá fiċiḋ púnt air; agus tá deiċ b-púnta ḋe orm. 4. Tá míle púnt ag Caoimġin O'Tuaċail orm-sa. 5.

IDIOMS.

b-fuil mórán aige air do ḋearḃraċair? 6. ni b-fuil nid air biṫ aige air, aċt tá cúig céad púnt ag feidlim air. 7. b-fuil airgead air biṫ aige-rean ort? 8. ni b-fuil, aċt píċe púnt air ċapall. 9. do bí céad go leiṫ púnt agam orra-ran araon. 10. ni b-fuil mórán orm—aċt amáin go b-fuil cion agur mear ag na daoinib orm.

OBS.—The learner who has carefully studied the foregoing exercises will see the difference in idiomatic meaning of air (contained in orm, *on me*), in the former and in the latter part of this last Example.

Another idiom, different from the foregoing, but which has been referred to already, arises from the use of cad é? *what (is) it?* with the verb do beiṫ. Cad é a tá ort? *what (is) it that is on thee?* conveys in Gaelic the meaning of "what ails thee." Applied to persons, cad é with air, refers to sickness or ailing of some kind; cia meud refers to debt, as cad é a tá ort, agur cia meud a tá ort? *What is it ails thee and how much dost thou owe? lit.* What is it is on thee and what amount is on thee? Again, cia meud with air applied to things for sale refers to their price.

Observe how widely these three sentences differ in meaning, while in words they are nearly alike.

1. Cad é a tá ort? What ails thee?
2. Cia meud a tá ort? How much dost thou owe?
3. Cia meud a tá air an eudaċ? What is the price of the cloth?

Explanation of cia, *what*; cad, *what*; cá, *where,* and meud, *amount.* Cia is an interrogative pronoun, as cia h-é? *who (is) he?* The verb ir is here omitted as it often is in short sentences. Ciᴀ usually aspirates the mutable consonant which follows it. It enters into a great many familiar expressions, such as ciᴀ ᴀip bic, who at all (ᴀip bic, *in life*.)

Cᴀᴅ might be considered a neuter form of ciᴀ; as, cᴀᴅ é ſin, what is that? cᴀᴅ ſá, what for? (ſá is a preposition, and means for or under); cᴀᴅ ſac? what (is) the reason? Why?

Cá, *adv.* where; *pron.* what; as, cá h-áic, what place? cá b-ſuil cú, where art thou? (pronounced quickly in conversation as if "*kowl thoo*)," cᴀ h-ᴀm, what time?

Meuᴅ (sometimes written méiᴅ) is the root of meuᴅuiġ, increase, enlarge, as in ʒo meuᴅuiġiᴅ ᴅiᴀ cú, may God increase you, i.e., that is, make you great or happy, increase your health and wealth. Meuᴅ signifies size, amount, quantity, number; as, ᴀn meuᴅ ᴅᴀoineᴀᴅ, the number of people, ᴀn meuᴅ ᴀipʒiᴅ, the amount of silver.

IDIOMS WITH Le.

2. Besides the idiomatic meaning conveyed by Le with the assertive verb iſ as denoting ownership, which has been already explained, page 47, there are other idioms which shall now be explained.

The verb iſ is always used in connection with Le, except where Le denotes being alone or being "by one's self," Leiſ ſéin as before shown p. 52.

Le with the verb iſ denotes: firstly, being in possession of, in the power of, on the side of, of one's party; secondly, regarding the mind

IDIOMS.

which is one's own and with it the thoughts of the intellect, will, fancy, hopes, fears, &c. With tá it signifies (1.) being *alone*, as tá tú leat féin, you are by yourself: (2.) being in favour of, as; o' iompuiġ an máġ, tá ar báire ro linn. i. e., the trump has changed, this goal is with us (*in our favour*.)

EXERCISE XIII.

1. Ir liom-ra an teać, ir leat-ra an talaṁ, ir leo-ran an teać aġur an talaṁ, aġur ir linne an doṁan mór. 2. An leir-rean an teać? ir leir é. 3. Aġur an talaṁ? Ní leir. 4. An leat-ra an capall aġur an leat-ra an bó? 5. Buḋ liom-ra an capall aġur an bó aġur buḋ leat-ra an talaṁ. 6. Níor liom an teać aġur níor leat-ra an ġort. 7. Cia leir an teać aġur cia leir an talaṁ? 8. Cia leir tú, a ṁic? 9. Ní linne an teać ro no an talaṁ rin. 10. Ní linn féin rinn féin, ir le Dia a tá rinn.

OBS.— The preposition le or ler comes after the interrogative pronoun, as above, cia leir an teać? (who) with whom the house? (whose is the house?) le becomes ler (generally spelled leir) before a vowel, and must be distinguished from the prepositional pronoun leir, with him, already shown.

THE VERB do beit.

EXERCISE XIV.

Mion-ḟoclóir.

áirnéis, cattle, chattel.
cóir, just, right.
a ḋuine cóir, oh, just man! equal to "my good sir."
deirḃṡiúra, *gen.* of deirḃṡiúr, a sister.
gamain, a calf, a yearling; gamana, *pl.*
leanḃ, a child.
malrac, a man-child. of from two to ten years old.
naoiḋeaṅ, naoiḋeaṅán, } an infant. *dim.* of nae, a human being (*obs.*)
páisde, páisdín, } a babe, a young child

seanataiṙ, a grandfather.
seanṁátaiṙ, a grandmother.
The terms ataiṙ mór, grandfather, and mátaiṙ mór, grandmother, are also in use.
timcioll, round, about.
ṫart timcioll, all round about, in view.
tír grád, tír gráda, *gen.* patriotism, love of country.
muintir an tír gráda, the patriotic party.

1. A ḋuine cóir, cia leis an teac so agus an áirnéis, agus an áit so go h-uile? 2. Is lem' ṡeanataiṙ an teac, is liom féin an áirnéis agus an áit a tá ṫart timcioll. 3. Agus an naoiḋeaṅán—cia leis é? 4. Mac mo ḋeirḃṡiúra. 5. An le muintir an tír gráda tusa? 6. Ní le muintir air bit rinn, is le Dia aṁáin rinn air rad. 7. An liḃ-se na gamana agus na h-uain, na caoiris agus an

IDIOMS. 75

ᴀipnéip úᴅ ɡo h-uile? 8. buṅ le'p peanacṫaip aɡup ap n-aċaip iaᴅ, aċt ní linn péin iaᴅ anoip. 9. buṅ lem' aċaip an malpaċ a connaipc tú a n-ᴅé. 10. Ip liom péin an páipᴅe úᴅ.

There is another very important class of idioms in connection with the verb ᴅo beiṫ (in the forms ip and buṅ) and the preposition le to which attention should be directed.

These idioms relate to the action of the intellect, the will, the memory, the imagination, fancy, and at times of the passions.

1. The intellect: the verb ip or buṅ with le is used in attributing knowledge; as, ip eol liom, It is knowledge with me (I know).
2. The will, choice, election, selection; as, ip toil liom, it is a wish with me (I wish); ip poɡa liom, it is a choice with me (I choose), ip mian liom, I desire; ip cuma liom, it is (a matter of) form with me, I am indifferent.
3. The memory, ip cuiṁin liom; it is memory with me I remember.
4. Imagination: ip ᴅeap liom, It is pretty with me (I think it pretty); ip ᴅeipe liom, I deem it prettier; ip peápp liom, I think it better, I prefer; ip olc liom, I deem it bad; ip meapa liom, I think it worse, I am very sorry for, I deem it a greater object of pity.

An example of this last idiom is a very simple sentence, ip maiṫ ṅam é, aċt ní maiṫ liom é; *lit.* It is good for me (ᴅam) but it is not good with me (liom.) Here the first clause may be translated literally, but the second is idiomatic, and signifies *I do not like it* (though, perhaps, it is good for me).

OBS. Conversely such English sentences as, I am aware; I wish; I intend, hope, expect; I think well, or ill, or much, or more, or little, or less of a thing; I prefer, deem pitiable, important, excellent, preferable; I like, choose; I feel surprised, delighted, &c.; also it *seems* good or bad, right or wrong,

76 THE VERB do beiṫ.

hard or soft, painful or pleasant, easy or difficult *to one*, must be translated according to idiom, as shown in the foregoing forms, with Le.

NOTE.—The principle on which this idiom is founded is that Le conveys the idea of connection, possession, right to anything, or power to dispose of it, party, relation to any subject matter.

The idea of preference and the like is expressed by adjectives in the comparative degree with Le, as feáṗṗ, better; annfa, dearer; ɒilre, fonder, &c.

Exercise XV.
Examples of Idiom.

English.	Literal.	Irish.
I prefer gold to silver.	It is better with me, gold than silver.	Iſ feáṗṗ Liom óṗ ioná aiṗ-ẓeaɒ.
I pity that man more than the other.	It is worse with me that man than the other man. (that is more deserving of pity)	Iſ meaſa Liom an feaṗ ſin ioná an feaṗ eiLe.
I think it sweet.	It is sweet with me.	Iſ miLiſ Liom.
If you like.	If it is good with thee.	Má'ſ maiṫ Leaṫ.
Are you willing to come with me?	Whether (is it) a will with thee to come with me?	An toiL Leaṫ teaċt Liom?

IDIOMS.

Don't you remember that day?	Is not a remembrance with you on that day?	Naċ cuimin liḃ an lá pn?
Do you wish to walk?	Whether (is) a desire with thee to walk?	An mian leat siúbal?
I like this place.	It is a pleasure with me this place.	Is áil liom an áit so.
I suppose you do (like).	It is a supposition with me that it is (a pleasure, &c., *und.*)	Is dóiġ liom gur ab eaḋ.
I would have chosen it.	It would be a choice with me.	Ba ṙoġa liom é.

Exercise XVI.

annsa, dearer
(*comp.*) of ionṁuin.
faġail, to get, find.
fan, stay.
fanaċt, } to stay,
fanaṁain, } *inf.*

fiona (*gen.*), of wine;
an fiona ól, of the drinking of wine.
teaċt, to come.

1. Is mian liom eolas d' faġail. 2. An fearr leat teaċt ann so ioná ḋul ann súd? 3. Is annsa liom fanaċt mar a tá mé. 4. Is mian liom fearsa gluarsaċt, go cuan ceapt an fiona ól. 5. An fearr

leat ranact ann ro ioná ṫul a baile? 6. iṫ cuma liom. 7. má'ṫ maiṫ ḋam an niḋ ṫin, ní maiṫ liom é. 8. iṫ áil liom ṫo ċáinṫ. 9. iṫ olc liom é beiṫ maṫ a ṫá ré. 10. iṫ olc an niḋ é ṫin ṫo ḋeiṁin.

OBS. The learner will notice the difference of idiom in the two last sentences. iṫ olc liom means I think it bad; that is, I have pity; iṫ olc an niḋ means it is a bad thing.

NOTE. Remember that the ṫ in ṫam, &c., is generally aspirated after a vowel or aspirated consonant, and after ṫ. ṫá, two, is usually aspirated ḋá, in the same way, or when beginning a sentence.

EXERCISE XVII.

bána, white
(*pl.* of bán).

bláṫaiḃ, blossoms
(*dat. pl.*) of bláṫ.

cuiṁin, } remem-
cuiṁne, } brance.

cumaṫ, power.

ṫúil, a desire, longing.

Éiṫeann, *gen.* of Éiṫe, Ireland.

muinṫiṫ na h-Éiṫeann, people of (the) Ireland.

ráṫṫaṫ, is found, is got.

leaṁnaċṫ, new milk.

léiṫean, a lesson.

léiṫean ṫ'ráṫail, to receive a lesson.

leinḃ (*voc.*), child,
a leinḃ mo ċroiḋe, child of my heart

maiṫ, a good.

míle maiṫ, a thousand good returns, thanks.

meuḋuiṫ, increase.

ṫo meuḋuiṫiḋ ṫia ṫo ċáil, may God increase your repute.

ṫéim, sway.

iṫ ionṁuin leaṫ mo ṫéim, you like all belonging to me.

ṫamṫaḋ, summer.

'ré, iṫ é, it is it.

'ré ṫin le ráḋ, that is to say.

reanfocal, a proverb.

rṫéiṫ, the firmament.

IDIOMS.

1. A ataip, ir mian liom léigean d'págail.
2. Tá go mait, a ṁic, ir bpeág liom-ra go b-ruil dúil agat 'r an b-pógluim. 3. Ir áil liom-ra an pógluim. 4. Dud bpeág le muintir na h-Éipeann an t-eolar. 5. An áil leat an obair a tá piaċtanaċ le léigean d'págail? 6. A ataip, ir áil liom. 7. Tá pean-pocal ann, "ní págtap léigean agur leaṁnaċt;" agur "Má'r ionṁuin leat mé, ir ionṁuin leat mo péim." 8. 'Sé pin le pád, má'r ionṁuin liom eolar, ir ionṁuin liom an obair. 9. Ir mait tú, a leinb mo ċpoide, beid eolar agat pór. 10. B-puil leabap agat? 11. Tá ód leabap agam. 12. Cia aca ir poga leat? 13. Ir peárr liom an leabap ro ioná an leabap pin. 14. Tóg an leabap ir annra leat. 15, Ir dear linn aṁarc aip an b-peup glar, aip na bláṫaib bána, agur aip an rpéip. 16. An cuiṁin lib an t-am ro, bliadain ó poin? 17. Ir cuiṁin linn. 18. So é an ramrad ir peárr a táinic le pice bliadain. 19. Go meuduigid Dia do cáil agur do cumar. 20. Go paib míle mait agat.

Section II.

The learner has already perceived that in the connection of words with each other, such as adjective with noun, verb with nominative, &c., the arrangement required by the idiom of the Gaelic is, as a rule, different from that followed in English.

The rules regulating this connection of words belong, strictly speaking, to Syntax; yet as even the simplest sentence requires some application of them, it is thought well to explain here the leading rules, before proceeding further. Exercises on Syntax as a whole shall be reserved for another place, but such idioms as the learner will most frequently meet, and with which he has already some acquaintance, will now be considered.

Thus the special object of this book will be attained, and the learner will be made acquainted with all the forms of ꝺo beiṫ, and enabled to arrange words in their proper order before proceeding to Declension and Conjugation.

The adjective and noun, verb and nominative case, &c., shall be treated of only as regards their relative positions. Rules regarding gender, inflection, &c., are held over.

I. IDIOMS OF THE ADJECTIVE AND NOUN.

The adjective follows the noun, which it qualifies, as ꝼeaṙ maiṫ, a good man; except

1. Numeral adjectives, both cardinal and ordinal: as, tṙí ꝼiṙ, three men; an ċeuꝺ leaḃaṙ, the first book.

When the number is higher than ten, and not a multiple of ten, the noun is put between the two words of which the numeral in such cases is always composed: as tṙí ꝼiṙ ꝺeuꝼ, thirteen men ; τρί bliaṫna ṗiċeaḋ, twenty-three years. In naming Sovereigns we sometimes use the cardinal number (not ordinal), but the more general method in such cases is to use the ordinal number : as, an ḋara henṗí, the second Henry, Henry II.

2. Some monosyllabic adjectives which are generally compounded with the noun so as to form but one word : as, ḋeaġ-ḋuine, a good man.

The principal of these are—ḋeaġ, good ; droċ, bad, raoḃ, evil, rean, old, which always precede the noun maiṫ, olc, aoroa, which have the same meaning, follow the noun. It is not unusual to find other monosyllabic adjectives sometimes preceding the noun : as, áṙḋ, buan, ḋaoṙ, ḋearḃ, ḋian, ḟíoṙ, ġeáṙṙ, ġlan, maoṫ, móṙ, naoṁ nuaḋ, óġ, ṫṙom, and some others.

Note.—The predicate, whether a noun or an adjective, precedes the noun when the assertive verb iṙ, or any of its forms, is employed in ascribing an attribute or quality to the noun, as iṙ maiṫ an ṙġeul é it is a good story. This is an emphatic form, and in it the adjective suffers no change whatsoever.

Here maiṫ is not the qualifying adjective in the ordinary sense—the statement made qualifies ṙġeul: iṙ is impersonal. But in iṙ rean maiṫ é, he is a good man, &c., the adjective qualifies the noun.

IDIOMS.

Exercise I.

buan-ċara, a lasting friend.
Colla, Coll, Culla, a man's name.
críona, shrewd, prudent.
Éireann, (*gen.*) Éirinn, (*dat.*) Ireland.
Niall, Niall, Neil.

1. Fear mór, láidir, treun. 2. Tá deaġ-ḋuine agur fear fairḃir ann. 3. Do ḃí an dara Niall 'na ṗíġ annr an am rin. 4. Do ḃí ceitre fir deug annr an d-tíġ rin. 5. An ceud agur an dara leaḃar ġaeḋilġe. 6. Do ḃí ré 'na ṗíġ or Éirinn trí bliaḋna riċead. 7. Ir ġlic an fear é, an feanduine críona. 8. Ir mé do ḃuan-ċara Colla. 9. Buḋ ré ard-ṗíġ na h-Éireann é. 10. An fean-ḟear liaṫ agur an bean aorda críona.

Obs.—Where a verb ascribes a quality to a noun, the adjective denoting that quality is unchanged and does not agree with the noun: as, tá an bean maiṫ, the woman is good—not tá an bean ṁaiṫ which would mean simply "the good woman is——" leaving the qualification still to be filled up. Also in the same way we say do ṗiġne ré an rcian ġeur, he made the knife sharp, or he *made sharp* the knife; where the adjective forms as it were part of the verb, and does not agree in any way with the noun Do ṗiġne ré an rcian ġeur (aspirating ġ of ġeur to agree with the feminine noun rcian) would signify "He made the sharp knife," and thus convey a different meaning.

II. IDIOMS OF THE VERB AND NOMINATIVE CASE.

The verb immediately precedes the nominative case, as ḃí mé, *I was.*

The nominative case must immediately follow the verb, and no word can be inserted between them. In the case of ıp or those particles which carry its force we have such sentences as, ıp mait ıaᴅ; they are good, where the adjective mait comes next the verb. ıp is in reality impersonal, and has no expressed nominative case. The emphasis is on mait. The quality is more prominent in the mind than the thing.

OBS. When the nominative is a pronoun, it may be joined to the verb as shown in the synthetic forms of ᴅo ḃeit.

There is no agreement between the verb and its nominative.

The synthetic forms are no exception to this rule. In them the pronoun is joined to the verb, *as a termination*, so that the nominative case still follows the verb.

When the nominative is a noun or nouns, the analytic form only can be used, which does not change in person or number. There is a change, however, in the present and future tenses indicative, after the relative pronouns ᴀ and naċ, which require the ending ap to be added to the present tense and pap to the future, but no change in person or number. Where a collective or plural noun is nominative to a verb, an agreement is often made to take place in the third person plural by the use of the synthetic form together with the noun which is the nominative.

Exercise II.

béarrar, (*rel. fut.*) (who) will give.
Donncaḋ, Donogh (Denis).
gealaċ, the moon.
ġearrar, (*past*) I cut.
leanaḋar, they followed.

lonnraċ, shining.
meur, a finger.
margaḋ, a bargain, a market.
ólar (*rel. pres.*) (who) drinks.
ráḋ, a saying.

1. Do ḃí ḃrian, Lorcan, aġur Donncaḋ ann. 2. Ir ḃreáġ an lá é ro ġo ḋeiṁin. 3. Má'r raḋa an lá, tiġ an oiḋċe. 4. An té naċ ólar aċt uirġe, ní ḃeiḋ ré airmeirġe. 5. Leanaḋar na ḋaoine é. 6. Tá an ġrian lonnraċ aġur ḃeiḋ an ġealaċ ġeal. 7. Air maiḋin a n-ḋé, ḋo ġearrar mo ṁeur. 8. An rear a ḃéarrar margaḋ mór ḋaoiḃ-re. 9. Tá na ba aġ ḋul ḋo'n aonaċ a márċ. 10. Deir na ḋaoine ġo ḃ-ruil ḃrian 'na rear ráir-ṁait, ġur mait an rcolaire é; aġur ir ríor an ráḋ rin.

III. IDIOMS OF THE GENITIVE CASE.

The genitive case comes next after the governing noun, and never before it, as láṁ an rir, the man's hand.

IDIOMS

When two nouns come together signifying different things the latter is put into the genitive case, for this reason the infinitive mood of verbs, being a verbal noun, takes the genitive case after it.

But in compound nouns, formed of two substantives, each word is still in the nominative case, and inflected according to the declension of the second word; as, Laṁ-ópo, a hand-sledge; *plural*, Laṁ-óipo, hand-sledges. There are, however, compounds, such as ꝼeap-ꝼeapa, a man of knowledge, in which the second part is in the genitive case according to rule. See "Second Book," pp. 38-40.

NOTE.—Nouns referring to the same thing are in the same case. [See "Second Book," p. 40, &c., for rules regarding aspiration in genitive case of proper names, and rules for family names.]

EXERCISE III.

Mion-ꝼoclóip.

bacul, a crozier.

pápaic na m-bacul, Patrick of the Croziers.

ban, *gen. pl.* of bean, a woman.

Sliab na m-ban, the mountain of the women.

Colum-Cille, Columba, or Columkill, i.e., the Dove of the Church.

cruinne, the universe.

domain, *gen.* of doman, the world.

ápo-tiżeapna an domain, supreme lord of the world.

Dúileaṁ, the Creator.

dúl, *gen. pl.* of duil, a creature, an element.

Dúileaṁ na n-dúl, the Creator of the elements

eappac, spring.

Éipeannac, Irish, an Irishman.

eipiġ, rise.

éirg, *pl.* of iarg, a fish.

feir, a parliament.

fir-feara, *gen.* of feap-feara, a man of knowledge.

í, an island.
1 Coluim-Cille, the island of Colum-kill.
Laoiḋ, a poem, a lay.
mapa, *gen.* of muiṗ, the sea.
oiṗḋeaṗc,, illustrious.
Oiṗín, Oisin, (Ossian.)
ṗíl, *gen.* of ṗiol, seed.
aġ cuṗ ṗíl, setting (*lit.* putting) seed.

talṁan, *gen.* of talaṁ, the earth.
topaḋ na talṁan, the fruit of the earth.
Teaṁaiṗ, Teaṁṗaċ (*gen.*), } Tara
tóġ, built, founded.
topaḋ. fruit.
Tiṗ na n-óġ, the land of the youths, or the land of youth.

1. Coṗ an ṗiṗ, aġuṗ láṁ na mná. 2. Leaḃaṗ an ṗiṗ-ṗeaṗa. 3. Sliaḃ na m-ban. 4. Topaḋ na talṁan aġuṗ éiṗġ na mapa. 5. Do ḃí ṗé aġ cuṗ ṗíl annṗ an Eaṗṗaċ. 6. Iṗ ṗé aṗ o-Tiġeaṗna, Dúileaṁ na n-oúl, áṗo-tiġeaṗna an ooṁain, aġuṗ áṗo-ṗiġ na cṗuinne. 7. Buḋ ṗé Colum-cille, naoṁ oiṗḋeaṗc Éiṗeannaċ, oo tóġ aiṗ o-túṗ cill ṁóṗ í Coluim-cille. 8. Eiṗiġ, a Oiṗín! oeiṗ páoṗaic na m-baċul. 9. Feiṗ Teaṁṗaċ ġaċ tṗeaṗ ḃliaḋain. 10. Laoiḋ Oiṗín aiṗ Tiṗ na n-óġ.

OBS. When two nouns come together in construction the article can be used *only* with the second; and even if the second does not admit of the article it cannot precede the first noun, as above coṗ an ṗiṗ, the foot of the man. We could not say an ċoṗ an ṗiṗ. This rule is worth attention, and is universal except when the word is a compound as above: an ṗiṗ-ṗeaṗa, of the man of knowledge.

4. IDIOMS OF THE DEMONSTRATIVE PRONOUN.

The demonstrative pronouns ro, this, ṕın, that, and ṕúo or úo, that yonder, come after the noun, and require the article to go before it: as, ᴀn ṕeᴀṕ ro, the man this, i.e., this man.

If the noun be accompanied by adjectives, they follow it immediately, the demonstrative pronoun coming last.

Exercise IV.

áilne (*pl.*), beautiful.   mᴀice (*pl.*), good.
bṕuᴀc, a brink.   ṕṕocán, a streamlet.
bṕuᴀc ᴀn c-ṕṕocáin, brink of   ṕṕocáin, *gen.*
  the s reamlet.   call, yonder.
oeᴀṕᴀ (*pl.*), pretty.

1. ᴀn ouıne uᴀṕᴀl ṕın. 2. Nᴀ mná oeᴀṕᴀ áilne ro. 3. Nᴀ oᴀoıne mᴀice ro. 4. ᴀ beᴀn jo ṕioṕ ᴀıṕ bṕuᴀc ᴀn c-ṕṕocáın! 5. Ƒeuc ᴀn ṕeᴀṕ úo call, nᴀc móṕ ᴀn ṕeᴀṕ é. 6. Iṕ ṕeáṕ lıom ᴀn ṕeᴀṕ bocc ṕın ıoná ᴀn ṕeᴀṕ ṕᴀıobıṕ úo. 7. Céıo ᴀmᴀc ᴀṕ ro. 8. Céıo ᴀnn úo ᴢuı ᴀn o-cıᵹ. 9. Cıᴀ h-é ᴀn ṕeᴀṕ jo? Iᴀ h-ıᴀo ṕúo? 10. Iṕ mᴀıc ᴀn ṕeᴀṕ úo; ṕ mᴀıc nᴀ oᴀoıne ıᴀo ṕúo.

OBS. These pronouns are indeclinable, but are sometimes chang d to suit the final vowel of the word which they ollow: as, ro into ṕe, ṕeo or ṕı, ṕın into ṕoın or ṕᴀn, which owe er is not re ommended. These pronounns must be are ully distinguished from the emphatic suffixes ṕᴀ ṕᴀn, e, &c., shown on p 37.

Exercise V.

alpaḋ, devouring.
an-ṁóıṗ (*dat. fem.*), very great.
baınṗeaḋ (who) would pluck out.
beıṫeaċ, a beast.
ġaċ uıle beıṫeaċ, every beast.
caṗaċtaċ,) (*gen.*) a
caṗaċtaıġe) cough.
cıa b'é, whoever.
cíocṗaċ, hungry.
cnáṁ, a bone.
coṗṗ, a crane.
dıan, vehement.
duaıṗ, a reward.
ṗıaclaıḃ, teeth.
pat. pl. of ṗıacaıl,
ıdıṗ m'ṗıaclaıḃ, between my teeth.

ṗóıṗıċın,) (to) help.
ṗóıṗeaċt,)
ġeall, promised.
ġeaṗṗaḋ, (to) cut.
ġlaoḋ, (he) called.
ġṗeamuıġ, stuck fast.
meıṗneaċ, courage.
neaṁḃuıḋeaċ, thankless.
onóıṗ, honour.
péın, (*dat.*) pain.
ṗıġneaṗ, I did.
náṗ ṗıġneaṗ maṗ ṗın, that I did not do so.
ṗáıṫ, (he) thrust.
ṗcóṗnaċ, the throat.
ṗġṗeaḋ, roar.

An ṗaol-ċú aġuṗ an Coṗṗ.

Am do ḃí ṗaol-ċú ġo cíocṗaċ aġ alpaḋ caoṗaċ noċ do ṁaṗḃ ṗé, do ġṗeamuıġ cnáṁ ḋí ġo daınġean ann a ṗcóṗnaċ, noċ do ċuıṗ a b-péın an-ṁóıṗ é. Do ṗġṗeaḋ ṗé ġo dıan, aġuṗ do ġlaoḋ ṗé ġo h-áṗd aıṗ ġaċ uıle beıṫeaċ ṗan maċaıṗe ṗóıṗıċın aıṗ. Do ġeall ṗé duaıṗ do ṫaḃaıṗt do cıa b'é a baınṗeaḋ an cnáṁ amaċ ar a rcórnaċ. Do ġlac an Corr meirneaċ iarraċt do ḋeunaḋ; do fáit rí a muineul fada ríor aġur do tarrainġ rí amaċ an cnáṁ. Dúḃairt rí an tan rin ġur dóiġ léi ġo m-beiḋeaḋ an faol-ċú rearṁaċ d'a focal, aċt iar n-deunaḋ caraċtaiġe dó, 'ré reo a dúḃairt ré—"Níor dóiġ liom a ċorr neaṁḃuiḋeaċ ġo m-beiḋteá ġan náire air biċ mar rin: b'féidir dam do ċeann a ġearradaḋ dó' ṁuineul 'nuair do ḃí ré idir m'fiaclaiḃ, dá m-buḋ toil liom, aġur ir cóir duit a ḃeiṫ buiḋeaċ díom, air ron nár riġnear mar rin leat."

Má ġnidir maiṫ do ḋuine diomḃuiḋeaċ, ir cóir duit-re a ḃeiṫ buiḋeaċ dé muna n-deunfaḋ ré docar duit.

KEY TO EXERCISES.

The corresponding English of those exercises of which the translation has not been given (*omitting the fables*), will serve as a useful series of graduated exercises in Irish composition. The learner who has carefully studied the books so far will have little difficulty in re-translating these exercises into Gaelic, and comparing them with the originals, according to which they are numbered for reference. The various forms of the verb bo beit shall not be given here. They will be found in the table, p 32, 33 and 34, and have been already explained.

PART I. SECTION I.

EXERCISE II.—1. Art thou well? 2. I am not sick. 3. The son is not young, but he is healthy. 4. This is the man who has (*at whom is*) the large hound. 5. The man and the woman, and the young son, (whether) are they well? 6. They are well (in health), but they are not young nor tall. 7. He says that I am young yet. 8. If you are not good, you are not prosperous. 9. Is the woman pretty? 10. She is very pretty, and she is a good woman (*is good the woman she*).

Ex. III.—1. Is the day long? 2. The day is long. 3. Teig says that the day is not long. 4. Dermot says that the day is long. 5. Are you certain that the day is long? 6. I am certain that the day is long. 7. Is the son young, and is he healthy and tall? 8. The son is young, and he is healthy, but he is not tall. 9. Is thy friend, Lorcan, fair and tall, big and healthy? 10. He is fair and tall, young and big, but he is not healthy.

Ex. IV.—1. Brian is a poor man, and he is healthy. 2. Morrogh is a rich man, but he is not healthy. 3. I am a young man, and I am humble. 4. That is a good story (*is good the story that*) indeed. 5. Thomas is a strong man, and he is healthy. 6. Nora is poor, but 'tis she that is prudent. 7. Peter and Patrick are big, but they are not cunning. 8. Hail! (lit. *it is thy life*) is it thou who art there (*in it*)? 9. It is I who am here (*in this*), it is true that I am here. 10. (The) love of my heart (art) thou.

Ex. V.—1. You are (*hab.*) there (*yonder*) often. 2. Teig says that they are (*do be*) in the town every day. 3. He is not there, but he is (*hab.*) in that house every week. 4. Are you (usually) healthy? 5. I usually have (*there is* (*hab.*) *with me*) good health, thanks (be) to (*with*) God. 6. They are not always well. 7. He (*assertive*) is a rich man now, and he is generous, as are his brothers. 8. You are (*sing.*) sick now, but you are not (*hab.*) ailing. 9. A fool has luck (*there is* (*hab.*) *luck on a fool*). 10. If you are poor, be patient.

Ex. VI.—1. Whether (*is it*) me, is it you, is it he? 2. (*It is*) not we, not you, not they. 3. Is it not (*neg. int.*) he, is it not she, is it not they? 4. Whether (*is it*) you who are there? 5. It is thou who art there. 6. Am I not a fine man? 7. You are not a bad man (*not bad the man thou*). 8. Are they not fine men? 9. It is they who are there. 10. Is she not a pretty woman? (*Is it not pretty the woman she?*)

Ex. VII.—1. Is not this a fine day? (*whether not fine the day it this?*) 2. It is a fine day indeed. (*Is fine the day it.*) 3. This morning is fine. 4. Brian is a good man; Mary is a good woman. 5. It is better late than never. 6. If (*it is*) slow it is sure, the vengeance of God. 7. It is better prudence than strength. 8. Better (is) the good which is than the good which was. 9. You say that better (is) the good which is than the good which was. 10. I say myself that this day is fine.

Ex. IX.—1. Art thou in good health? 2. I am, thanks (be) to (*with*) God. 3. He says that I am not well. 4. I am (*hab.*) in the town every day. 5. Do the men be long-lived in that place? 6. They do (be) indeed, but they do not be so healthy as we are. 7. If we are not so rich as they are. 8. Ye are (*hab.*) in that city often. 9. We are (*hab.*) often there (*yonder*). 10. Ye are poor, but ye are cunning men (*it is cunning the men ye*).

Ex. X.—1. Is not this a fine night? (*whether not fine the night it this?*) 2. Brian says that yesterday was a fine day, and that to-day is a fine day (*that was fine the day, the day yesterday, and that* (*is*) *a fine day the day to-day*). 3. The hills are green, at a distance from us. 4. If they are green (they are) not grassy. 5. Is not Brian a learned man. 6. He is an expert scholar indeed. 7. We are learning Gaelic. 8. Ye are doing well. 9. We are (*hab.*) reading the first and second book (*gen.*) at (the) school in which we are. 10. That is a good story.

Section II.

Exercise II.—1. I was in the city to-day. 2. Were you at the rock. 3. I was not yet there. 4. (Whether) was the son young? 5. He says that you were good. 6. He was rich, but he was not good. 7. Teig says that they were not poor. 8. If you were not strong, you were cunning. 9. I am certain that she was not dead. 10. He was free.

Ex. IV.—1. I was to-day where (lit. *in a place*) I used be long ago. 2. They were the men who were on the street that time. 3. Whether (was) I the man who used be there? 4. I was not the man. 5. Used I to be there? 6. You used not be usually there. 7. Was it you (*pl.*) who used be there long ago? 8. Was it not (*whether not* [past]) yourself who used to be there? 9. It (was not) I indeed. 10. May it not be he? That thou mayst be safe.

Ex. V.—1. The assistance of God is nearer than the door. 2. Yesterday was a fine day. 3. Whether (is it) they who are there? 4. They are not the men, but they are the women who were there. 5. We are young and healthy, but they are rich. 6. Necessity has no law (*is not at, &c.*). 7. We used not to be so (*as this*). 8. I am (*hab.*) in good health, thanks to God. 9. They are not sick now, but they are weak yet. 10. Ye are young and strong.

Ex. VII.—1. (Whether) wert thou (*syn.*) at the rock? 2. I was not myself at the rock, although my people used to be in that place in time long since. 3. Used they be usually there? 4. He says that they were young. 5. That you (*sing*) may be well, and that you may be long-lived. 6. They were well (in health) but they were not rich. 7. I have not been (*I was not,* hab.) well since I left my own country. 8. You used to be going from town to town. 9. It is true that, indeed, but I was not yet in a place like this place. 10. Were ye not (*hab.*) at that time rich enough?

Ex. VIII.—Was his head gray? 2. His head was not gray that time, but it is gray now.

3. Are his eyes blue? 4. They are not, but they are brown. 5. You (*sing.*) are well now, and that you may be long so. 6. He was a good man, but not the man who is esteemed (*but not he the man on whom is esteem*). 7. Whether were ye in (*under*) esteem in this country? 8. We were not, for the prophet is not regarded (*there is not regard on &c.*) in his own country. 9. That saying is true indeed. 10. I was (*hab.*) rich that time, and thou usedst to be poor at (*in*) the same time. 11. There is no pleasure without misery. 12. It is better to be idle than badly employed. 13. Contention is better than solitude. 14. The haughty is (often) under (the form of) beauty. 15. A fool has luck. (*there is* (hab.) *luck on, &c.*). 16. There is not in this world but a mist. 17. Not lasting the warfare of friends. 18. The valiant does not (always) be lasting. 19. If I am poor, I have a generous heart. 20. Hunger is good sauce (*assertive form*). 21. Was this the man who was sick? 22. They say that he was, but he is not the sick man now. 23. He who is (*hab.*) idle is badly employed. 24. A friend in the court is better than a groat in the purse. 25. A wren in the fist (i.e. *in one's possession*) is better than a crane on loan (*or time*, i.e., *not yet caught.*)

Section III.

Exercise II.—1. I shall be in Limerick tomorrow. 2. I shall not be there until after tomorrow, but my brother was there the night before last. 3. He says they will not be (*anal.*) in the house. 4. They will be (*syn.*) in the house

certainly, and I (*emph.*) will be in the other house.
5. That is the man who will be going to Galway next week (*this week towards us*). 6. We shall be great yet. 7. The Gaelic will yet be in great esteem, in noble Erin, in (the) island of the kings. 8. Will you be going to the sea? 9. I will be. 10. Thou wilt be tall, and big, and healthy.

Ex. IV.—1. We would be far from the world. 2. He says that he would be satisfied with it. 3. You would not be ready at that time. 4. If I would not be (*unless I would be*), you could (*it were possible for you*) (to) walk by (*with*) yourself. 5. If I should wish (*if a wish should be with me*) to do that, perhaps you would not like it (*it were possible that it were not a pleasure with you it that*). 6. If they should be free, they would be satisfied enough. 7. If I had money (*if there should be money at me*) you would have it likewise. 8. If it would not be (for) this thing alone we would be in peace till this time. 9. We would be at home long since. 10. Ye would be there certainly.

Ex. VI.—1. Do not be hard, and do not be soft. 2. Have no fear (*let not fear be on you*). 3. Let there not be shame on ye. 4. Let not thy act be from thy tongue. 5. Be satisfied with that. 6. Let us be going hence (*out of this*). 7. Be honest in thy actions. 8. Let us be merry, and be ye not sorrowful. 9. Know ye (*let knowledge be with ye*) that that is right. 10. Let him be free.

Ex. VIII.—1. To be, or not (*without*) to be. 2. We have been (*we are after being*) at the large town. 3. Donal being asleep (*on being in his sleep of Donal*). 4. The men having been shut up in prison (*after *being of the men, &c.*) 5. They were on the point of being ruined. 6. The assembly being filled with the host. 7. It is a good thing to be humble. 8. He ordered the doors of the church to be shut. 9. That thing is to be done quickly. 10. He set (*put*) the seed to be increased (*for the purpose of being*).

Ex. IX.—1. Thank you (*that good may be to you*). 2. Well now, 'tis you are the man who is cunning. 3. I suppose it is (*a supposition is with me that it is*). 4. There is a man named Teig (*to whom is name Teig*) in that house now. 5. I suppose that I (am) the man who will be in the church. 6. Is it you who are there? (*whether thou who art there*)? 7. Yes, (*it is I*) indeed. 8. Are you well? 9. I am, thanks be to God. 10. I desired henceforth to proceed (*a desire was with me henceforth* (to) *proceed*). 11. Young and beautiful was she. 12. Is your mother alive yet? 13. (She) is not; she is dead long since. 14. Is this the man whose name is Felim? 15. No; his name is Kian. 16. Do you speak Irish? 17. I speak Irish, which is as sweet as honey. 18. I do not speak it yet, but I am learning that tongue. 19. (The) life of the historian (is) truth. 20. The life of man is his (own) will.

Part II. Section I.

Exercise V.—A. 1. Have you your book? (*is thy book with thee*). 2. I have my book and my pen. 3. Will you (*sing.*) be with me (*as one with me*) going to Limerick? 4. I shall be with thee (*in company with thee*) going to Limerick to-night. 5. Put your new hat on you. 6. Put your shoes on you. 7. Put your silken cloak (cloak of silk) about you. 8. There is a red cloak about him. 9. Speak with him. 10. I have a story for you.

B. 1. Be not afraid (*let there not be fear on you*). 2. What is your name (*what is name to you*)—Lorcan or Patrick? 3. Teig is my name. 4. Do good to them. 5. Stay with me here, and I will be together with thee immediately. 6. Do you own this house? (*whether with thee the house this*). 7. I do not own it, but that man owns it. 8. We will have rain. 9. It is raining (*at rain*). 10. It is not freezing.

C. 1. There is a mist. 2. There is not; it is snowing. 3. There is not in this world but a mist. 4. The mist is great which is there. 5. Give (to) me your hand. 6. Give me a kiss. 7. Come to (*towards*) me. 8. Do not run from me. 9. It is going over us. 10. Ye have silver and gold.

PART II. SECTION II.

EXERCISE II.—1. I have silver and gold. 2. Have you silk and satin (*whether is —— with thee*)? 3. She has green silk. 4. We will have silver and gold and land. 5. Have they silver and gold, house and land—friends and flocks? 6. Has she a dowry and land? 7. She has a dowry and land and cows. 8. The aged man has a young son and a pretty daughter. 9. He has a full purse and great wealth. 10. There is a long day with us, and we have silver and gold, land and flocks—glory (be) to God.

Ex. III.—1. I have a hound but it is not my own (*it is not with myself*). 2. We have silver and gold, but they are not ours. 3. Had Morrogh honey and meal, and were they his own? 4. He had honey and meal, and they were his own. 5. Will you have fresh butter and honey? (*will there be —— with thee*). 6. I will have fresh butter, and honey, and bread, but they will not be my own, but Morrogh's (*with &c.*). 7. Are the young son, and the large house, and the strong horse yours? (*whether with thee &c.*). 8. You say that they are mine, that large house is mine, and everything which I have. 9. There is great abundance with thee (*it is great the fulness which is with thee*). 10. It is well that I have them and that they are my own.

Ex. IV.—1. What is wanting from thee? (*what is from thee; what hast thou lost?*) or what are you seeking? 2. I want my hat; have you it? 3. I have it not, and I know not where it is. 4. I have silver, but it is not my own. 5. Whose is it? 6. It is my father's. 7. Whose (*who with*) that young child, and what is his name? (*is name to him*). 8. He is the man of the house's (son) (*it is with (the) man of the house he*), and Connor is his name. 9. That pretty young daughter is the woman of the house's (*with the woman of the house*), and Finola is her name. 10. If she should have that young woman as a daughter, she would be a happy woman.

Ex. V.—1. A hundred thousand welcomes to

you (*before thee*). 2. I have nine hundred thousand welcomes before thee. 3. Thou art dear to (*with*) my heart. 4. I have a true good friend. 5. He is a (in his) faithful good friend to me and it is he has great means (*it is with him is great wealth*). 6. Ye possess the riches. 7. It is they and your father who possess it (*it is with —— it is*). 8. 'Tis great the wealth you have. 9. Have you any Irish book (any—*in life*)? 10. I have the first and second book, and they are my own.

Ex. VI.—1. That house was mine (*was with me that house*). 2. Did you own (*whether (were) with thee*) the horse and the sheep? 3. My brother owns them. 4. You ought to have a horse for yourself (*it is right for thee, a horse to be with thee for thyself*). 5. I am here poor, miserable, without a horse or an ass to have for myself. 6. You will have a horse presently, and a house, land and flocks, lambs and sheep; and they all your own (*they all to thy own share*). 7. I am alone (*by myself*) now. 8. Thou wert alone that time. 9. She will be alone in the house. 10. We are alone on the world.

PART III. SECTION I.

EXERCISE III.—1. Are you cold (*is cold on thee*). 2. I am cold, and I was cold, and I fear (*there is fear on me*) that I will be cold. 3. Were ye sick (*was sickness on ye*)? 4. Yes; (*there was*) and I am glad we are not so now (*gladness is on me that it is not now on us*). 5. Will you be thirsty? (*will thirst be on thee*). 6. I will not be thirsty, for I am much better (*there is a great improvement on me*). 7. There is not heat or cold, sickness or disease at all on me—thanks (be) to God. 8. A good man has no sorrow or fear (*sorrow or fear do not be on a good man*). 9. May there be happiness and prosperity, and luck and good fortune on you. 10. I feel pleasure (*pleasure is on me*) to be talking to you.

Ex. IV.—1. Have you great regard for me? (*is great regard at thee on me?*) 2. Yes; (*there is*) and I have regard for (*on*) a good man. 3. Have you affection and regard for God? 4. I have, and I had (*there is and was* [with me]), and I will have affection and love for ever for Him, for He is my Father. 5. I have love for God and God has love for me. 6. See—is there fame and great esteem on thee? 7. There is—there is great repute on me in every place, and many people have regard for me. 8. My father and my mother had great love for me, and I have affection and love for my father and my mother. 9. I hope (*a desire is with me*) that there will not be sickness or disease, or sorrow, or breaking of heart on thee. 10. There is not; thanks (be) to God: farewell.

Ex. VI.—1. Are you greatly esteemed in this country? (*is great esteem on thee in the country this*). 2. Yes: (*there is*) and the people have affection and love for me. 3. Was there great love for your son and for your children among the people? (*in midst of the people*). 4. Yes; (*there was*) I say to (*with*) you that there was great regard for us, and that there will be respect for us, but there was not, and there is not yet, regard for our smooth, sweet mother-tongue. 5. It is bad (the thing it) disrespect to be on that (*a thing*) which is har-

monious, sweet-sounding. 6. You have sense
7. If I have sense, that report is not out on me.
8. Had you regard and affection for yourself? 9.
Every person has regard and affection for himself,
fondness and love for God and for our people
10. There is great repute on you; you are esteemed; no one dislikes you (*dislike is not at any one on thee*).

Ex. VIII.—1. Donal drunk and his wife drinking water. 2. A while drunk (*on drunkenness*), a while furious (*on fury*), tearing the strings (of the harps) and going mad. 3. On yesterday morning 'tis sorrowful I was. 4. On the top of the cliff overhead the coast. 5. My sorrow! that I am not on board (of a) ship; there I would be first-rate. 6. In badness or in excellence, I am as I am. 7. He is straying and wandering. 8. He put them on board. 9. It is better be going forward that going backward. 10. It is better to spare in the beginning than at the end. 11. O, old man, who art foolish (*on folly*). 12. On yesterday morning, before the sun, early.

Ex. IX.—1. Have you love for God? 2. Yes; (*there is* [at me]) and if you have love for God, God has love for you. 3. I have, I had, and I will have (*is, was and will be at me, &c.*), affection for ever for God. 4. That is a good story from the mouth of him who has knowledge on the soul of man that he is to be alive in the kingdom of God for ever. 5. Art thou a prophet? (*whether a prophet thou?*) 6. I am not a prophet, but I am a Christian. 7. Now, have you affection and love for your father and for your mother? 8. I have; (*there is*) for no one has love for God when he has not love for his own father and mother. 9. God ordained to (the) man, to have affection and love for his father, and for his mother, and a long life and prosperity is promised to him who has love for his own father and mother. 10. You are right: everyone has affection for the individual who gave the beginning of life to him. 11. Have you affection for yourself? 12. I have love and fondness for God first, for my country in the second place, for myself, for thyself, with thy permission, and for every good man. 13. You have enough (*your sufficiency*) there. 14. I wish every good man to have affection for me. 15. I desire thy affection to be on me.

Ex. XI.—1. Were you at the fair to-day? 2. I was. 3. What was the price of (*how much was on the [per] head of the*) horses? 4. There was a great price on horses, and on cows, but sheep were cheap enough. 5. Were oats, and wheat, and barley cheap there? 6. Corn was dear, but butter was cheap. 7. What is the price of tea and sugar in the large town? 8. They are cheap; and it is a good story that there is not too great a price on them now. 9. Is there a great price there now on silk, or on satin? 10. They are dear; but the price of (*which is on*) calico is small.

Ex. XII. Does your father owe much? (*is much on your father?*) 2. My father owes two hundred pounds, and I myself owe three hundred pounds. 3. I bought a horse at the fair yesterday; its price was fifty pounds; I gave forty pounds on it; and I owe ten pounds of it (*there are ten pounds of it on me.* 4. I owe Kevin O'Tual a thousand pounds(*a thousand pounds are at—on me*). 5. Does your brother owe him much? 6. He owes him nothing (*there is not a thing in life at him on him*), but he owes Felim five hundred pounds. 7. Do you owe him any money? (*has he anything on you*). 8. No; (*there is not*) but twenty pounds for a horse. 9. They both owe me a hundred pounds (*I have a hundred pounds on them both*). 10. There is not much on me, but only that there is regard and esteem with (*at*) the people for me.

Ex. XIII.—1. The house is mine (*is with me the house*), the land is thine, the house and the land are theirs, and the whole world is ours. 2. Is the house his own? (*whether with himself the house*) it is with him. 3. And the land? not his (*not with him*). 4. Was the horse yours, and was the cow yours? 5. The horse was mine and the cow, and the land was yours. 6. The house was not mine, and the field was not yours. 7. Whose (is) (*whe with*) the house, and whose is the land? 8. Whose (*child are*) you, son? 9. This house is not ours, nor that land. 10. Not with ourselves, ourselves (are in right), it is with God we are.

Ex. XIV.—1. Honest man, whose (is) this house, and the stock, and this place entirely? 2. The house is my grandfather's (*with—*); the stock is my own, and the place which is round about. 3. And the infant—whose (is) it? 4. My sister's son. 5. Do you belong to the patriotic party? (*whether with [the] people of the patriotism, you*). 6. We belong to no party at all, we belong to God alone, entirely. 7. Are the calves and the lambs, the sheep and that stock your own entirely?

8. They belonged to (*were with*) our grandfather and our father, but they do not belong to ourselves now. 9. The youth whom you saw yesterday is my father's (*with my father*). 10. That child is my own.

Ex. XVI.—1. I desire (to get) knowledge. 2. Do you prefer to come here or to go there? (*whether better with thee (to) come here than (to) go there*). 3. I would rather (*it is dearer with me*) stay as I am. 4. I desire henceforth to repair to the true haven of drinking wine. 5. Do you prefer to stay here or (*than*) to go home? 6. It is equal with me. 7. If that thing is good for me, I do not like it (*not good with me it*). 8. I like your talk. 9. I think it bad that he should be as he is (*it is bad with me he to be as he is*). 10. That thing is bad indeed.

Ex. XVII.—1. Father, I wish to get a lesson. 2. 'Tis well, my son, I think it good (*it is fine with me*) that you have a desire for (*in the*) learning, 3. I like (*the*) learning. 4. The people of Ireland thought well of knowledge (*it was fine with—the knowledge*). 5. Do you like the work that is necessary to get a lesson? 6. Father, I like (it). 7. There is a proverb " learning and new milk are not found," and, " If you like me you like my sway." 8. That is to say, if I love knowledge, I love the work. 9. Good you are, child of my heart, you will have knowledge yet. 10. Have you a book? 11. I have two books. 12. Which of them do you choose? (*which at them is choice with thee?*) 13. I prefer this book to that book. 14. Take the book you wish best. 15. We think it pretty to look on the green grass,

on the white blossoms, and on the firmament.
16. Do you remember (*whether remembrance with you*) (*pl.*) this time, a year ago? 17. We remember.
18. This is the best summer which came for (*with*) twenty years. 19. May God increase your fame and your power. 20. May a thousand thanks (*good*) be with you.

PART III. SECTION II.

EXERCISE I.—1. A big strong, valiant man.
2. A good man and a rich man are there (*in it*).
3. Niall II. was (in his) king at (*in*) that time. 4. Fourteen men were in that house. 5. The first and (the) second Irish Book. 6. He was (in his) king over Ireland twenty-three years. 7. He is a cunning man (*assertive*) the shrewd old man. 8. I am your lasting friend, Culla. 9. He was (*asser.*) high king of (the) Ireland. 10. The gray old man, and the shrewd aged woman.

Ex. II.—1. Brian, Lorcan, and Donogh were there. 2. This is a fine day indeed. 3. If the day is long, the night comes. 4. He who drinks but water will not be drunk. 5. The people followed him.
6. The sun is shining and the moon will be bright.
7. On yesterday morning I cut my finger. 8. The man who will give a great bargain to ye. 9. The cows are going to the fair to-morrow. 10. The people say that Brian is (in his) an excellent man, that he is (*asser.*) a good scholar; and that saying is true.

Ex. III.—1. (The) foot of the man and (the) hand of the woman. 2. (The) book of the man of knowledge. 3. Mountain of the women.

4. The fruit of the earth and the fishes of the sea.
5. He was sowing (*putting* [of]) seed in the spring
6. It is He, our Lord (is), Creator of the elements, Supreme Lord of the world, and Monarch of the universe. 7. It was (he), Columkill, an illustrious Irish saint, who founded first (the) great Church of I. Colum-kill. 8. Rise! O Oisin! says Patrick of the Croziers. 9. The Parliament of Tara (took place) every third year. 10. The poem of Oisin on the Land of youths.

Ex. IV.—1. That gentleman. 2. These beautiful pretty women. 3. These good people (*the people good* [*pl.*] *these*). 4. O woman there below on the brink of the streamlet. 5. See that man yonder, is he not a big man. 6. I prefer that poor man to (*than*) that rich man 7. Go out of this. 8. Go yonder to the house. 9. Who (is) he that man? who (are) those (yonder?) 10. That man is good, these people (yonder) are good.

The Society strongly recommend that those desirous of learning the Irish Language should lose no opportunity of speaking it, and endeavour to get the pronunciation from persons who have been accustomed to speak it.

The language being now taught in so many schools, there is no longer any difficulty in procuring a teacher, but even without the aid of any such, fair progress may be made by careful study of these three books.

The pronunciation of vowels and unaspirated consonants can be learned from the First Book; of the mutable letters from the Second. If any difficulty be found in applying these rules, the books may be read over to any Irish-speaking person and a correct pronunciation easily obtained,

VOCABULARY OF ALL WORDS IN THIS BOOK.

A, *intj.* (sign of vocative case) O.

A (*sign of inf.*) to.

A, *poss. pron.* his, her, its, their.

A, *rel. pron.* who which, whom, that, all that.

A (or ı), *prep.* in.

A, put for ᴀᵹ.

Ab (form of ıꞅ), may be, is.

Aca, *pr. pron.* at or with them; ciа аса, which of them.

Act, *conj.* but.

Aö, *n. m.* luck.

Ao', *pr. pron.* cont. for ann oo) in thy.

Aᵹ, *prep.* at, with.

Aᵹ, sign of participle.

Aᵹaıb, *pr. pron.* at ye.

Aᵹaıö, *n. f.* a face; aıꞅ aᵹaıö, forward.

Aᵹaınn, *pr. pron.* at us.

Aᵹam, *pr. pron.* at me.

Aᵹat, *pr. pron.* at thee, аᵹат-ꞅа, *emph. form.*

Aᵹuꞅ, *conj.* and.

Aıce, *adv.* hard by, near; аm' аıce, near me; 'nа аıcc, near him; 'nа h-аıce, near her.

Aıcı, *pr. pron.* at her.

Aıᵹe, *pr. pron.* at him; aıᵹe-ꞅeаn, *emph. form.*

Aıl *n. f.* will, pleasure.

Aıll, *n. f.* a cliff.

Aılle, *n. f. gen.* of a cliff.

Aılne, *adj. pl.* beautiful.

Aınm, *n. m.* a name.

Aıꞅ, *prep.* on, upon.

Aıꞅ, *pr. pron.* on him, it; aıꞅ-ꞅeаn, *emph. form.* aıꞅ ꞅéın, on himself. Aıꞅ ball, aıꞅ o-túꞅ, &c. See adverbial phrases. p. Sign of participle aıꞅ m-beıċ, on being.

Aıꞅᵹeаo, *n. m.* silver,

Airgio, *gen.* silver, money.
Aipnéir, *n. f.* stock, cattle, chattel.
Áit, *n. f.* a place.
Alp, *v. a.* devour.
Alpaṅ, *v. a. inf. and part.* devouring.
Áluinn, *adj.* beautiful.
Am, *n. m.* time; am ṅo ḃí, a time there was.
Am', *pr. pron.* (cont. for ann mo,) in my.
Amaḋán, *n. m.* a fool.
Aṁáin, *adv.* only, alone.
Aṁancup, *n. m.* success, good luck.
Aṁaic, *v. a. irr. inf.* (to) see.
An, *article,* the.
An, *int. partic.* whether.
An, *intens. partic.* very, anḋear, very pretty.
Anam, *n. m.* a soul.
Aníor, *adv.* up (from below).
Anlan, *n. m.* a condiment. ("*Kitchen.*")
An-ṁóip, *adj.* (*dat.*) very great.

An-ṁóp, *adj.* very great.
Ann, *prep.* in.
Ann, *pr. pron.* in him, in it.
Ann, *adv.* there.
Annr, *prep.* in.
Ann rin, *adv.* there (in that); then.
Ann ro, *adv.* here (in this.)
Ann ṗúṅ, *adv.* then, there, yonder.
Anoir, *adv.* now.
Annra, *comp. adj.* dearer.
Anjóg, *n. m.* misery.
Aoinfeact, one time; a n-aoin feact le, together with.
Aonaċ, *n. m.* a fair.
Aora, *adj.* aged, old.
Ap, *int. partic.* whether,
Ap, *poss. pron.* our.
Ap, *rel. pron.* (comp. of a and po) before past tense, who, what.
Apán, *n. m.* bread.
Apḃap, *n. m.* corn.
Apṅ, *adj.* high, tall.

árouǵ, *n. m.* a high king, a monarch.
árotiǵeapna, *n. m.* a sovereign lord.
á'ṛ, for aǵuṛ and; as.
aṛ, *prep.* out of, aṛ ṛo out of this.
aṛal, *n. m.* an ass.
ataiṛ, *n. m.* a father; ataiṛ móṛ, a grandfather.
átaṛ, *n. m.* gladness.
atṛuǵað, *n. m.* a change, removal.
b' see buð.
ba (*past tense of* iṛ), it was; see buð.
ba, *n. f. pl.* cows.
bacul, *n. m.* a crozier.
bað (buð) (*cond. of* iṛ), should be.
báið, *n. f.* love, affection.
bail, *n. f.* success, blessing, prosperity.
baile, *n. m.* a town, 'ṛa m-baile, *and* a baile, at home.
bainṛeað, *v.* (*cond.*) would pluck out.

bainne, *n. m.* milk.
báiṛe, *n. m.* a goal, a game.
baiṛeuð, *n. m.* a hat.
ball, *n. m.* a spot, a limb, a member. aiṛ ball, presently.
ban, *gen. pl.* of women.
bán, *adj.* white.
bána, *adj. pl.* white.
baoiṛ, *n. f.* folly.
báṛṛ, *n. m.* the top.
beaǵ, *adj.* little.
bean, *n. f.* a woman.
bean an tiǵe, *n. f.* woman of the house.
béaṛṛaṛ, *v. fut rel.* (who) will give.
beata, *n. f.* life. 'Sé ðo beata, *lit.* it is thy life; Ðia ðo beata, God is thy life—Hail!
beið, *v. fut, indic.* will be (also biaið.)
beiðeað, *v. cond.* would be.
beiðeaṛ, *v. fut rel.* (who) will be.

beiṫ, *n. f.* a being.
beiṫ, *v. inf.* to be.
beiṫeaċ, } *n. m.* a
beiṫiḋeaċ } beast.
beo, *adj.* living.
beul, *n. m.* a mouth.
bí, *v. imp.* be.
bí, } *v. past indic.* was,
biḋ, } were.
biaḋ, *n. m.* food.
biaiḋ. See beiḋ.
biḋ, *n. m. gen.* of food.
biḋ, } *v. hab.* do be,
biḋeann, } am usually.
biḋeaḋ, *v. imp.* let be.
biḋeaḋ, *v. hab. past.* used to be.
binn, *adj.* melodious.
bireaċ, *n. m.* increase, improvement.
biṫ, *n.f.* being, life; aip biṫ, at all, any in life.
blaṙoa, *adj.* sweet sounding.
bláṫ, *n. m.* a blossom.
bláṫaib, *n. m. dat. pl.* blossoms.
bliaḋain, *n. f.* a year.
bliaḋna, *n.f. pl.* years.

boċṫ, *adj.* poor.
boġ, *adj.* soft.
bonn, *n. m.* a groat.
borb, *adj.* fierce. haughty ; *n.* a haughty person.
bórḋ, *n. m.* a board ; aip bórḋ, on board.
braṫ, *n. m.* a cloak, a garment.
bráṫ, *n. m.* judgment ; go bráṫ, for ever ; never, till judgment.
breáġ, *adj.* fine, fair.
breoiṫe, *adj.* sick, ailing.
brian, *n. m.* Brian (Bernard).
briġ, *n.f.* essence, substance ; gan briġ, valueless.
brireaḋ, *n. m.* breaking ; brireaḋ croiḋe, heart-breaking.
bróga, *n. f. pl.* shoes.
brón, *n. m.* sorrow.
brónaċ, *adj.* sorrowful.
broṫaire, *n. m. nom.* *and gen.* a butcher.
bruaċ, *n. m.* a brink.

buaib, *n. f. dat. pl.* cows.

Ḃuail, *v. past indic.* struck.

buan, *adj.* lasting.

buan-capa, *n. m. and f.* a lasting friend.

buan-ṗaoġalaċ, *adj.* long-lived.

buḋ (*past tense of* iṗ), it was; ꞇo m-buḋ, that it may be.

buiḋeaċap, *n. m.* thanks, gratitude.

buile, *n. f.* rage, madness; aiṗ buile, raging mad.

bun, *n. m.* foundation, sole, bottom; aiṗ bun, established.

buṗ, *poss. pron.* your.

buṗ (buḋ) (*fut. of* iṗ), it will be.

Ca, see cia.

Cá, *int. partic.* where; ca h-áiꞇ, what place.

Caḃaiṗ, *n. f.* help.

Caḋ, *int. adv.* what.

Caḋáṗ, *n. m. gen. of* cotton.

Caḋáṗ, *n. m.* cotton.

Cáil, *n. f.* repute.

Caill, *v.* lose; ḋo ċaill ṗé, he lost.

Cailltean, *v. pass.* is lost.

Cáinꞇ, *n. f.* talk.

Cáiṗḋe, *n. f.* respite, time for payment; aiṗ ċáiṗḋe, on loan, or not yet obtained.

Cáiṗḋe, *n. pl. of* capa, friends.

Caoꞇaḋ, *ord. num.* fifty.

Caoiṁġin, *n. m.* Kevin.

Caoiṗiġ, *n. f. pl.* sheep.

Caoṗa, *n. f.* a sheep.

Caoṗaċ, *gen. of* a sheep.

Caoṗċaiḃ, *n. f. dat. pl.* sheep.

Capaill, *n. m. pl.* horses.

Capall, *n. m.* a horse.

Capallaiḃ, *n. m. dat. pl.* horses.

Capa, *n. m. and f.* a friend.

Capaḋ, *gen. of* friends.

Carcar, n. m. a prison.
Carn, n. m. a pile of stones, a cairn.
Carn-aoiliġ, n. m. a dungheap.
Carraig, n. f. a rock.
Carachtać, n. f. a cough.
Carachtaiġe, n. f. gen. of a cough.
Cataiṗ, n. f. a city.
Céaḋ, num. a hundred.
Ceann, n. m. a head. iaṙġ an ceann, fish per head.
Ceannuiġeaṙ, v. past. indic. I bought.
Ceaṗt, adj. right, just.
Céiḋ, num. (gen. of ceuḋ), first.
Céill, n. f. dat. sense.
Ceiṫṙe, num. four.
Ceo, n. m. a mist.
Ceuḋ, ord. num. first.
Ceuḋna, adj. same; maṙ an g-ceuḋna, as the same, likewise.
Cia, int. pron. who; cia leiṙ, whose? cia b'é, whosoever.
Cia meuḋ, how much.

Ciall, n. f. sense.
Ciallṁaṙ, adj. sensible.
Cian, n. m. Kian, a man's name.
Cill, n. f. a church.
Cille, n. f. gen. of a church.
Cinnte, adj. certain.
Ciocṙać, adj. hungry.
Cion, n. m. regard.
Cionn (ceann), a head; oṙ mo ċionn, over my head.
Ciṙḋe, n. m. a treasure.
Clainn, dat. children.
Clann, n. f. children.
Cláṙ, n. m. a board, a table.
Cliṙte, adj. expert.
Cloć, n. f. a stone.
Cloiċín, n. f. a pebble.
Cluinim, v. pres. I hear.
Cnáṁ, n. m. a bone.
Cneaṙḋa, adj. honest.
Cnoc, n. m. a hill.
Cnoic, pl. hills.
Co, see coṁ.
Cocán, n. m. straw.
Coḋlaḋ, n. m. sleep, ann a ċoḋlaḋ, asleep.

Cogaó, n. m. war.
Coigilt, v. inf. to spare, sparing.
Coileać, n. m. a cock.
Cóimdeaćt, n. f. attendance, protection; a g-coimdeaćtle, in company with.
Cóip, adj. right, just. Iſ cóip duit, you ought.
Coipce, n. m. oats.
Coiſe, gen. of a foot.
Colla, n. m. Coll.
Colum-cille, n. m. Columkille.
Com, or co, adv. so, as, prefix, together.
Cómnuide, n. m. an abode; a g-cómnuide, always.
Concubap, n. m. Connor.
Connaipc, v. irr. past. saw.
Copp, n. f. a crane.
Cop, n. f. a foot.
Copamlaćt, n. f. a likeness, a similitude.

Cpíona, adj. shrewd, prudent.
Cpíoptaid, n. m. a Christian.
Cpoide, n. m. a heart.
Cpóit, v. past. indic. shook, flapped.
Cpuaid, adj. hard.
Cpuinne, n. f. the Universe.
Cpúipcín, n. m. and f. a pitcher, a small jar.
Cpuitneaćt n.f. wheat.
Cú, n. m. and f. a hound.
Cuain, gen. of a coast.
Ćualap, v. irr. past. I heard.
Cuan, n. m. a coast, harbour.
Ćugainn, pr. pron. towards us, to us.
Ćugam, pr. pron. towards me, to me.
Ćuici, pr. pron. towards her, to her, to it.
Cuid, n. f. share, portion; dod' ćuid féin, to your own share.

Cúig, *num.* five.

Cuimin, Cuimne, } *n. f.* remembrance, memory.

Cuir, *v.* put, send.

Cuir, *v. past. indic.* put, sent.

Cuirid, *v. pres.* puts; go g-cuirid sé, that he may put.

Cuirfead, *v. cond.* would put or send.

Cúirt, *n. f.* a court.

Cúl, *n. m.* the back; air g-cúl, backwards.

Cum, *n.* order, in order that; used as a *prep.* aspirated by do understood before it: governs *genitive.*

Cuma, *n. m. and f.* a form (or shape); (used *adjectively*), equal, indifferent.

Cumar, *n. m.* power.

D', for do, thy, do, to, and de, of, and sign of past tense and infinitive.

Dá, *conj.* if.

Dá, *num.* two.

D'a, *cont.* for do a, to whom, to which, to his, of which, &c., of (those) whom.

Daingean, *adj.* strong, firm.

Daingean, *n. m.* a fortress.

Dam, *pr. pron.* to me.

Daoine, *pl.* people.

Daoineaḋ, *gen. pl.* of people.

Daoinib, *dat. pl.* people.

Daor, *adj.* dear.

Dar, *prep.* by.

Dar, for do ar, to our.

Dar for do a ro, to which was, &c. (with past tense.)

Dara, *ord. num.* second.

Dar ab, or da n-ab (form of ir), to whom or which is, i.e. do a n-ab, n, euphonic.

Dar b' (do a ro bud), to whom was.

Daṫ, *n. m.* colour.

De, *prep.* of, off, from.

Dé, *pr. pron.* off or from him.

Dé, yesterday, a n-dé.

Dé, *gen.* of Dia, of God.

Deaġ, *adj.* good.

Deaġduine, *n. m.* a good man.

Deaġ-ṗac, *n. m.* good luck.

Dearb, *adj.* real.

Dearbráċair, *n. m.* a real brother.

Dearbráiṫre, *pl.* real brothers.

Dearg, *adj.* red.

Deas, *adj.* pretty.

Deasa, *adj. pl.* pretty.

Deiċ, *num.* ten.

Deiṁin, *adj.* certain; go deiṁin, indeed.

Deiṗ, *v.* say, says.

Deirbṡiúr, *n. f.* a sister (a real sister).

Deirbṡiúra, *n. f. pl.* sisters.

Deireaḋ, } *n. m.* an
Deire, } end;
fa ḋeireaḋ, at last.

Deirim, *v.* I say.

Deiṡe, *comp. adj.* prettier.

Deo, } *n. f.* (obs.) an
Deoiġ, } end (diaiġ) used only in fa ḋeoiġ, at last: go deo, for ever, &c.

Deorać, *adj.* sorrowful.

Deuġ, *num.* (ten); teen.

Deun, *v. irr.* do, make.

Deunaḋ, *v. inf.* (to) make; aġ deunaḋ, doing.

Deunar, *v. rel.* (who) does.

Deunfaḋ, *v. irr.* should do.

Deunta, *pass. part.* done, made.

Di, *pr. pron.* of her, to her, off her, or it.

Dia, *n. m.* God.

Diaiġ, *n. f.* (obs.) an end; used in a n-diaiġ, after; am' ḋiaiġ, after me; 'na diaiġ, after her; diaiġ a n-diaiġ, after each other.

Dian, *adj.* vehement.
Diaṗmuiꙋ, *n. m.* Diarmuid, Dermot.
Dilir, *adj.* fond, dear.
Dilre, *comp. adj.* fonder.
Diogalcar, *n. m.* vengeance.
Diomaoin, *adj.* idle.
Diomburꙋeać, *adj.* thankless.
Dipeać, *adj.* straight, sure.
Diu, to-day; a n-ꙋiu, or a n-iuꙋ.
Olige, }
Oligeaꙋ, } *n. m.* law.
Do, *poss. pron.* thy.
Do, *prep.* to.
Dó, *pr. pron.* to him.
Do, to; sign of infinitive mood.
Dob', for ꙋo buꙋ, it was (before a vowel).
Doćaṗ, *n. m.* loss, damage, hurt.
Doꙋ', *pr. pron.* to thy.
Dóiḃ, *pr. pron.* to them.
Dóiꙋeunca, *adj.* impossible.

Dóig, *n. f.* a supposition.
Doilgior, *n. m.* sorrow.
Doilgior croiꙋe, sorrow of heart.
Doirṗe, *pl.* doors.
Dom', *pr. pron.* to my.
Domain, *gen.* of the world.
Doman, *n. m.* the world; an ꙋoman uile, the whole world.
Dóṁnall, *n. m.* Donal
Dona, *adj.* wretched.
Donn, *adj.* brown.
Donnćaꙋ, *n. m.* Donogh, Denis.
Dorar, *n. m.* a door.
Dorn, *n. m.* a fist.
Dorcaꙋ, *v. inf.* (to) spill.
Dreoilín, *n. m.* a wren.
Droć, *adj.* bad.
Droć-gnócać, badly employed.
Droć-ṁear, *n. m.* contempt.
Droć-ṗiać, *n. m.* bad fortune.

Duais, *n. f.* a reward.
Dubaipc, *v. irr.* (past) said.
Dúil, *n. f.* a longing.
Duil, *n. f.* a creature, an element.
Dúileaṁ, *n. m.* the Creator; Dúileaṁ na n-dúl, Creator of the elements.
Duine, *n. m.* a person, a man.
Duic, *pr pron.* to thee.
Dul, *v.* (*inf.*) (to) go, going.
Dúl, *gen. pl.* elements.
Dúnca, *part.* sheet.
é, *pers. pron.* he, him, it.
eaḋ, *pron.* form of é; an eaḋ, forsooth; 'reaḋ, it is (yes); ní h-eaḋ, it is not (no); maireaḋ, &c.
eaḋar, *prep.* between. (*See* ioir.)
eaḋrainn, *pr. pron.* between us.
eaġla, *n. f.* fear.
earraċ, *n. m.* spring.
eile, *adj. pron.* other.

eire, *n. f.* Erin, Ireland.
éireann, *gen.* of Erin.
éireannaċ, *n. m.* an Irishman.
eiriġ, *v.* rise.
éirinn, *dat.* (in) Erin.
eirg, *pl.* fishes (*nom. s.* iarg).
eicill, *v.* fly; d'eicill ré, he flew.
eoin, *n. m.* John.
eol, } *n. m.* knowledge.
eolar, }
érean, *pers. pron. emph.* he, himself.
euḋaċ, *n. m.* cloth.
euḋaċ-caḋáir, *cpd. n. m.* calico (cloth of cotton).
euḋan, *n. m.* a face.
fá, *prep.* far, under.
faḋ, *n. m.* length; a b-faḋ, far; aip faḋ, entirely; faḋ ó, long since.
faḋa, *adj.* long.
fáġ, *v.* leave; d'fáġ (*past*) left.
fáġ, *v. irr.* find, get.

Fágail, v. inf. (to) get.
Fágtap, v. pass. is found, is got.
Fáið, n. m. a prophet.
Fáilte, n. f. a welcome.
Fairge, n. f. the sea.
Faitċeap, n. m. fear.
Falluing, n. f. a mantle.
Fan, v. stay.
Fanaċt, panamuin, v. inf. (to) stay.
Fann, adj. weak.
Fán, n. m. straying.
Faoi, prep. under.
Faolċú, n. m. a wolf.
Faṫ, n. m. cause; aip faṫ, because; cpeud faṫ, wherefore.
Feabap, goodness; aip peabap, first-rate; dul b-peabap, improving.
Feap, n. m. a man; Feap-tiġe, a householder; Feap an tiġe, man of the house.
Feapaib, dat. pl. men.
Feap-feapa, cpd. n. m. a man of knowledge.

Feapg, n. f. anger.
Feapp, comp. adj. better; ip feapp, best; do b'feapp, it were better; ip feapp liom, I prefer.
Feaptainn, n. f. rain.
Feapoa, adv. henceforth.
Féidip, adj. possible; ip féidip dam, I can.
Feidlim, n. m. Felim.
Féin, emph. pron. self, own.
Feip, n. f. a parliament.
Feoil, n. f. flesh, meat.
Feola, gen. of meat.
Feuċ, v. irr. see, look.
Feupmap, adj. grassy.
Fiacail, n. f. a tooth.
Fiaclaib, dat. pl. teeth.
Fiappuiġim, v. (first pers. pres. ind.) I ask, enquire.
Fial, adj. generous.
Fiċe, num. twenty; dá fiċid, two score.
Fiċead, num. twenty.
Fion, n. m. wine.
Fiona, gen. of wine.

Fıonn, *adj.* fair, white.
Fıonnġuala, *n.f.* Finola.
Fíoṗ, *adj.* true.
Fíoṗ-uirġe, *n.m.* spring water.
Fíoṙ, *n. m.* knowledge.
Fıṙ, *gen.* of a man, *pl.* men.
Fıṙ-ṗeaṙa, *gen.* of a Seer.
Fiṙınne, *n.f.* truth.
Focal, *n. m.* a word.
Foclóıṙ, *n. m.* a dictionary.
Fóġluım, *v.* learn ; aġ ṗóġluım, learning.
Fóġlumṫa, *adj.* learned.
Foġuṙ, *adj.* near ; a b-foġuṙ, near.
Foıġıoeaċ, *adj.* patient.
Fóıl, *n.f.* a while ; ṗo ṗóıl, for a while.
Fóıṙıṫin, } *v.* (*inf.*),
Foıṙeaċṫ, } (to) help, helping.
Fom', *pr. pron.* under my.
Fonn, *n. m.* delight, an air, pleasure.
Fóṙ, *adv.* yet.
Fuaċṫ, *n.f.* cold.
Fuaıṙ, *v. irr.* (*past*), found, got.
Fuaṫ, *n. m.* hatred.
Fuıl, *v.* (sec. form of ṫá) is, are.
Fúm, *pr. pron.* under me.
Ġaċ, *adj. pron.* each, every ; ġaċ uıle, every ; ġaċ n-aon, every one.
Ġaeḋılıġ, } *n.f.* Gaeḋılġe, } lic ; the Irish language ; also the Highland Scotch.
Ġaıllıṁ, *n.f.* Galway.
Ġáıṙoeaċaṙ, *n. m.* gladness.
Ġalaṙ, *n. m.* disease.
Ġaṁan, *n. m.* a calf.
Ġaṁana, *pl.* calves.
Ġan, *prep.* without ; ġan a beıṫ, not to be (sign of *neg. inf.*)
Ġaṙoa, *adj.* spruce, clever, neat.
Ġé, } *n. m. and f.* a goose.
Ġéaḋ, }

Ɣeal, *adj.* bright, white.
Ɣealać, *n. f.* the moon.
Ɣeall, *v.* promise; ġeall (*past*), promised; maṗ ġeall aiṗ, because, in consequence of.
Ɣeallta, *part.* promised.
Ɣean, *n. m.* affection.
Ɣeaṗṗ, *adj.* short.
Ɣeaṗṗ, *v.* cut.
Ɣeaṗṗaḋ *v.* (*inf.*) (to) cut.
ġeaṗṗar, *v.* (*past.*) I cut.
Ɣiḋ, *conj.* though.
Ɣioṗṗa, *comp. adj.* shorter, nearer.
Ɣlac, *v.* take; ġlac (*past*), took.
Ɣlan, *adj.* clean, pure.
Ɣlaoḋ, *v.* call, cry; ġlaoḋ (*past.*) called.
Ɣlaṗ, *adj.* green.
Ɣlic, *adj.* cunning.
Ɣlóiṗ, *n. f.* glory.
Ɣluaracṫ, *v.* (*inf.*) (to) go, to proceed.

Ɣnáṫ, *n. m.* usage, custom; ve ġnáṫ, usually.
Ɣné, *n. f.* form, sort, appearance, kind.
Ɣniḋiṗ, *v. irr.* thou dost.
Ɣnioṁ, *n. m.* an act.
Ɣnioṁaṗtaiḃ, *dat. pl.* acts.
Ɣnóṫać, *adj.* busy.
Ɣo, *prep.* to, towards, till; no Ɣo, until Ɣo v-ṫí, unto.
Ɣo, *conj.* that (particle before verbs).
Ɣo, sign of adverb.
Ɣoiv, *v.* steal; ġoiv, *past.* stole.
Ɣoṗm, *adj.* blue.
Ɣoṗt, *n. m.* a field.
Ɣṗáḋ, *n. m.* love.
Ɣṗáin, *n. f.* dislike, disgust.
Ɣṗáinne, *n. m.* a grain; ġṗáinne v'óṗna, a grain of barley.
Ɣṗeamuiġ, *v.* stick; vo ġṗeamuiġ, stuck fast.

Ɠɼeim, *n. m.* a bit, a morsel; ɠɼeim ꝼeola, a piece of meat.

Ɠɼéin, *n. f. dat.* the sun.

Ɠɼian, *n. f.* the sun.

Ɠuꞃ, form of ɠo, with past tense.

Ɠuꞃ, *conj.* that; ɠuꞃ mé, that (it is) I.

Ɠuꞃ ab (form of iꞃ) that it is; may be ɠuꞃ ab eaꞿ, that it is.

Ɠuꞃ, *prep.* (form of ɠo) unto.

I, *prep.* in.

Í, *pers. pron.* she, her, it.

I, *n. f.* an island.

Í-ꞃe, *pers. pron. emph.* she.

Iaꞿ, *pers. pron.* they, them.

Iaꞿꞃan, *pron. emph.* themselves.

Iaꞃ, *prep.* after; iaꞃ m-beiṫ, after being, having been (sign of participle.)

Iaꞃꞃaċt, *n. f.* an attempt.

Iaꞃꞃaiꝺ, *v. (inf.)* (to) seek, seeking; aɠ iaꞃꞃaiꝺ biꝺ, in search of food; ꝺ'iaꞃꞃaiꝺ, asking.

Iaꞃɠ, *n. m.* a fish.

Iḃ, *pers. pron.* you, ye.

Iḃꞃe, *pron. emph.* yourselves.

Iꝺiꞃ, *prep.* between.

Im, *n. m.* butter.

Imꞃeaꞃ, *n. m.* strife.

Inġean, *n. f.* a daughter.

Iniꞃ, *n. f.* an island.

Inn, *pers. pron.* we, us.

Inne, *pron. emph.* ourselves.

Innte, *pr. pron.* in her.

Iom, *intens. prefix,* many.

Iomaꞃcuiꝺ, *n. f.* too much.

Iomlán, *n. m.* the entire.

Iompuiġ, *v.* turn, change.

Ion, *prep.* in.

Ion, particle expressing fitness.

Ioná, *conj.* than; also written iná and 'ná.

1onṁuin, *adj.* beloved.
1ſ, *v.* (assertive) it is (used as sign of superlative).
Lá, *n. m.* a day.
Labaıſi, *v.* speak; do labaıſi (*past*) spoke.
Labſiaım, *first pers. pres.* I speak.
Labſiann, *hab.* speak.
Laʒ, *adj.* weak.
Láıdıſi, *adj.* strong.
Láṁ, *n. f.* a hand.
Láṁ-óſid, *n. m.* a hand sledge.
Lán, *adj.* full.
Lán, *n. m.* the full, plenty.
Laoıó, *n. f.* a lay, a poem.
Láſi, *n. m.* the midst; a Láſi, in the midst; aıſi Láſi, laid low.
Le *prep.* with.
 sign of inf. Le beıċ (for) to be.
Leabaıſi, *gen.* of a book.
Leabaſi, *n. m.* a book.
Leaṁnacc, *n. m.* new milk.

Leanadaſi, *3rd. pers. past.* they followed.
Leanb, *n. m.* a child.
Leac, *pr. pron.* with thee; ſlán leac, farewell, leac-ſa, *emph.*
Leaċ, *n. f.* a half.
Leaċ-ṁaſib, *adj.* half-dead.
Led' *pr. pron.* with thy.
Léı, ⎫ *pr. pron.* with
Leıċe, ⎭ her.
Léıʒead, *inf.* (to) read, (aʒ—) reading.
Léıʒean, *n. m.* a lesson.
Léım, *n. f.* a leap.
Léım, *v.* leap.
Leınb, *voc.* child.
Leıſi, (Leſ form of Le) with.
Leıſ, *pr. pron.* with him.
Leıſean, *pron. emph.* with him.
Leıſſin, *pron.* with that.
Leıċ, *dat.* half; céad ʒo leıċ, a hundred and a half.
Lem', *pr. pron.* with my.

Leo, *pr. pron.* with them.

Leoṗ (or Lóṗ,) *adj.* sufficient.; ɪr Leoṗ Lıom, I think it enough; ꝛo Leoṗ, sufficiently, in plenty.

Leoran, *emph. form* of Leo.

Le'ṗ, with our.

Leun, *n. m.* affliction.

Lıaċ, *adj.* gray.

Lıneuoaċ, *n. m.* linen cloth, linen.

Lınn, *pr. pron.* with us.

Lınne, *emph. form* of Lınn.

Lıom, *pr. pron.* with me; Lıom-ra, *emph. form* Lıom féın, by myself.

Lıonta, *part.* filled.

Lıtıṗ, *n. f.* a letter.

Lóġmaṗ, *adj.* precious.

Loınꝛe, *gen.* of a ship.

Lonꝛ, *n. f.* a ship.

Lonnṗaċ, *adj.* glittering, shining.

Loṗcan, Lorcan.

Lorꝛ, *n. m.* a track.

Luımneaċ, *n. f.* Limerick.

Luımnıġ, *dat.* Limerick.

Luaċ, *n. m.* a price.

Lúṫġáıṗ (and Luaṫġáıṗ,) *n. f.* laughter, gladness.

Má, *conj.* if.

Mac, *n. m.* a son.

Máö, *n. m.* a trump.

Maoaö, Maoṗaö, } *n. m.* a dog.

Maıoın, *n. f.* morning.

Máıṗe, *n. f.* Mary.

Maıreaö, *conj.* well, if so; má ır eaö, if it is it.

Maıṫ, *adj.* good; ꝛo maıṫ, well.

Maıṫ, *v.* forgive.

Maıṫ, *n. f.* a good, a favour; mıle maıṫ, a thousand thanks.

Maıṫe, *adj. pl.* good; *n. pl.* the nobility.

Mall, *adj.* slow; ꝛo mall, slowly, late.

Malṗaċ, *n. m.* a boy a man-child.

Maoin, n. f. wealth, means.
Maoċ, adj. soft.
Mar, conj. aṡ; mar ṙo, mar ṡın, so; mar ṡın ꞇe, however, accordingly; mar a, where; mar aon ꞇe, together with.
Mara, gen. of the sea.
Márać, n. m. morrow; a márać, to-morrow; aċṙuġaṫ a márać, after to-morrow.
Marḃ, adj. dead.
Marḃ, v. kill; ꞇo ṁarḃ ṙé, he killed.
Marġaṫ, n. m. a market, a bargain.
Má'ṡ (má iṡ) if it is.
Máċarṫa, adj. maternal.
Mé, pers. pron. I, me,
Meaṫon, n. m. the middle; meaṫon-ꞇae, mid-day; meaṫon-oıṫċe, midnight.
Mearḃal, n. m. error; aıṙ mearḃal, astray

Mear, n. m. esteem.
Mearra, comp. adj. worse.
Mearaṁaıꞃ, adj. estimable.
Mearġ, n. m. midst (used as a cpd. prep.) a mearġ amongst.
Mearuıġċe, part. adj. esteemed.
Méıꞃo, n. f. quantity; ca ṁéıꞃo (Munst.) how much. See meuꞃo.
Meıṡġe, n. f. drunkenness, aıṙ meıṡġe, intoxicated.
Meıṡneać, n. m. and f. courage; mıṡneaċ, id.
Meuꞃo, n. m. quantity, cıa ṁeuꞃo, how much.
Meuꞃuıġ, v. increase.
Meuꞃuıġıṫ, third pers. pres. increase, ġo meuꞃuıġıṫ Ꞇıa ċú, may God increase you.
Meuꞃuıġċe, part. adj. increased.
Meuṙ, n. m. a finger.
Mıan, n. m. desire.

Mil, *n. f.* honey.
Míle, *num.* a thousand.
Míle, *n. m.* a mile.
Milıɼ, *adj.* sweet.
Min, *n. f.* meal.
Min, *adj.* fine.
Minic, *adj.* frequent.
ɼo minic, oftentimes,
Mion, *adj.* small.
Mion-ꜰoclóıɼ, *n. m.* a vocabulary.
Miɼe, *n. f.* frolic, aıɼ miɼe, in a frolic.
Miɼe (meɼı), *pron. emph.* I, myself.
Mná, *pl.* women, *gen.* of a woman.
Mnaoı, *dat.* (to) a woman.
Mo, *poss. pron.* my.
Mó, *comp. adj.* more, larger, greater.
Moċ, *adj.* early, ɼo moċ.
Móɼ, *adj.* great, large.
Móɼán, *n. m.* many, móɼán ɒaoıneaò, many people.
Muıneıl, *gen.* of a neck.
Muıneul, *n. m.* a neck.

Muıntıɼ, *n. f.* people.
Muna, *conj.* unless, if not.
Munaɼ, form of muna with past tense.
Muɼċaò, *n. m.* Morrogh, Morty.
Na, *art. pl.* and *gen. sing. fem.* the.
Ná, *neg. par.* sign of *imp.* do not.
'Ná, than (for ıoná).
'Na, in his (for ann a).
Naċ, *rel. pron. neg.* who not, that not; *int.* whether not.
Naċaɼ, form of Naċ with past tense.
Nae, see naoıòeán.
Náıɼe, *n. f.* shame.
Naoıòeán, ⎱ *n. m.* an
Naoıòeanán, ⎰ infant, from nae, *obs.* a human being, and nán diminutive.
Naoı, *num.* nine.
Naoṁ, *n. m.* a saint.
Náɼ, form of naċaɼ, that not, that may not, whether not.

'Nᴀp, in our (for ᴀnn ᴀp.)
Ne, *emph. suffix. with pl. prons.*
Neᴀċ, *pron.* one, anyone.
Neᴀṁbuıḋeᴀċ, *adj.* thankless, ungrateful.
Neᴀpᴛ, *n. m.* strength.
Ní, *neg. par.* not.
Nıᴀʟʟ, *n.m.* Niall, Neill.
Nıḋ, *n. m.* a thing.
Ní h-eᴀḋ, *par. & pron.* it is not, nay.
Ní'ʟ, contracted for ní ḃ-ꜰuıʟ, is not.
Níop, form of ní, with past tense.
Níoꞃ, (i.e. nıḋ ıꞃ), sign of comparative.
No, *conj.* or, nor.
Noċ, *rel. pron.* who, which, before ıꞃ, or past tense.
Noċᴛ, *n.* (*obs.*) night; ᴀ noċᴛ, to-night.
Nópᴀ, *n. f.* Nora.
Nuᴀḋ, *adj.* new.
'Nuᴀıp, (for ᴀn uᴀıp) when. (*lit.* the hour.)

Ó, *prep.* from.
O, (form of uᴀ,) a descendant.
Obᴀıp, *n. f.* work.
Ocꞃᴀꞃ, *n. m.* hunger.
Óg, *adj.* young.
Oıḋċe, *n. f.* night.
Óıp, *prep.* for.
Óıp, *gen.* of gold.
Óıꞃḋeᴀpc, *adj.* illustrious.
Oıꞃín, *n. m.* Oisin.
Óʟ, *v.* drink, ᴅ'óʟ ꞃé, he drank; ᴀg óʟ, drinking.
Óʟᴀꞃ, *rel. form.* (who) drinks.
Oʟc, *adj.* evil, bad.
Oʟcᴀꞃ, *n. m.* badness.
Óm', *pr. pron.* from my.
Onóıp, *n. f.* honour.
Óp, *n. m.* gold.
Opᴀıḃ, *pr. pron.* on ye.
Opᴀınn, *pr. pron.* on us.
Ópḋᴀ, *adj.* golden.
Óꞃᴅuıg, *v.* order, ordain, ᴅ'óꞃᴅuıg ꞃé, he ordained.
Opm, *pr. pron.* on me.
Ópnᴀ, *n. f.* barley.

Oppa, *pr. pron.* on them.
Opparan, *emph.* form of oppa.
Opc, *pr. pron.* on thee.
Opcra, *emph.* form of opc.
Or, *prep.* over, cionn, overhead, above *(with gen.)*
Pádraic, *n. m.* Patrick.
Páiroe, *n. m.* a child.
Páiroín, *n. m.* a little child.
Peaoap, *n. m.* Peter.
Peann, *n. m.* a pen.
Péin, *dat.* pain, a b-péin, in pain.
Pian, *n. f.* pain.
Póg, *n. f.* a kiss.
Preacán, *n. m.* a crow.
Púnt, *n. m.* a pound.
Púnta, *pl.* pounds.
Ráo, *n. m.* a saying.
Ráo, *v. (inf.)* (to) say.
Raib, sec. form of bí, was.
Rac, *n. m.* prosperity, luck

Re, *prep.* with.
Réio, *adj.* ready, plain.
Réim, *n. f.* sway; péip, *dat.* (of puap, will) in *cpd. preps.*; as a péip, oo péip, according to (with *gen.*)
Réip, (a péip,) last night; acpuğao a péip, the night before last.
Reubao, *part.* tearing (to tear.)
Riaccanac, *adj.* necessary.
Riaccanap, *n. m.* necessity.
Rig, *n. m.* (also píoğ or pí), a king; na puğ, of the kings.
Rigeact, *n. f.* a kingdom (also píoğact.)
Rigne, *v. irr.* (past) did, made.
Rigneap, *v. irr.* I made, I did.
Ric, *v.* run.
Ro, *par.* with past tense.

Ró, *intens. par.*, very, too much.
Ró-ḃeaṙ, very pretty.
Roġa, *n. f.* a choice.
Róiṁ, *prep.* before.
Róṁaṫ, *pr. pron.* before thee.
Ró-ṁóp, *adj.* very great.
Ruġ, *v. irr.* (past) took, bore.
Sa, *suffix*. emphatic particle.
'Sa, for anṅṙ an, in the.
Saiḃḃiṙ, *adj.* rich.
Saiṫ, *v.* thrust; ḋo ṙáiṫ ṙé, he thrust.
Sáiṫ, *n. f.* sufficiency.
Saiṁṙaḋ, *n. m.* summer.
San, *suffix*. emphatic particle.
Saob, *adj.* false, bad.
Saobġṙáḋ, *n. m.* foolish or misplaced love.
Saoġal, *n. m.* the age, the world.
Saor, *adj.* free, cheap.

Saṙ-ṁaiṫ, *adj.* exceedingly good.
Sároa, *adj.* contented.
Sáruiġ, *v.* satisfy; ḋo ṙáruiġ (*past*), satisfied.
Scáṫ, *n. m.* a shadow.
Scáṫa, *gen.* of a shadow.
Scian, *n. f.* a knife.
Sciaṫáin, *gen.* of a wing.
Sciaṫán, *n. m.* a wing.
Scoil, *n. f.* a school.
Scolaiṙe, *n. m.* a scholar.
Scóṙnaċ, *n. m.* a throat.
Sé, *pers. pron.* he, it.
Se, *suffix*. emphatic particle, also ṙi.
Sé, *num.* six.
'Sé, for iṙ ṙé, it is it.
Seaċ, *prep.* beside, by
Seaċrán, *n. m.* straying, error.
Seaċṫṁain, *n. f.* a week.
Seaḋ (for iṙ eaḋ) it is, yes.
Seal, *n. m.* a while.
Sean, *adj.* old.

Seɑn, form of ꞅɑn.
Seɑnɑċɑıꞃ, *n. m.* grandfather, also ɑċɑıꞃ móꞃ.
Seɑnꞃuıne, *n. m.* an old person.
Seɑnꝼeɑꞃ, *n. m.* an old man.
Seɑnꝼocɑl, *n. m.* a proverb (old word); also ꞅeɑnꞃáꞅ, old saying.
Seɑnṁáċɑıꞃ, *n. f.* a grandmother; also máċɑıꞃ móꞃ.
Seɑnóıꞃ, *n. m.* an elder.
Seɑꞃc, *n. m. & f.* love.
Seɑꞃc-ġꞃáꞅ, *n. m.* intense love.
Seɑꞃṁɑċ, *adj.* steadfast.
Seo, see ꞅo.
Seoꞅ, *n. m.* a jewel.
Séꞃeɑn, *pron.* emph. form of ꞅe.
Seun, *n. m.* prosperity.
Seunṁɑꞃ, *adj.* prosperous.
Sġéıṁ, *n. f.* beauty; ꝼɑoı ꞃġéıṁ, under (*the form of*) beauty.

Sġeul, *n. m.* a story.
Sġꞃeɑꞅ. *v.* shriek, roar.
Sġꞃıob, *v.* scratch.
Sġꞃıobɑꞅ, *v.* (inf.) (to) scratch, scratching.
Sġꞃıoꞃcɑ, *part. adj.* ravaged, devastated.
Sı, *pers. pron.* she, it.
Sıɑꞅ, *pers. pron.* they.
Sıɑꞅꞃɑn, emph. form of ꞃıɑꞅ.
Sıꞇ, *poss. pron.* you, ye.
Sıꞇꞃe, emph. form of ꞃıꞇ.
Sıl, *gen.* of seed.
Sın, *dem. pron.* that.
Sín, *v.* stretch.
Sıneɑꞅ, *v.* (inf.) (to) stretch, stretching.
Sınn, *pers. pron.* we, us.
Sınn ꝼéın, *pron.* ourselves.
Sınne, emph. form of ꞃınn.
Sıoc, *n. m.* frost, ɑġ ꞃıoc, freezing.
Sıoꞅɑ, *n. m.* silk, bꞃɑꞇ ꞃıoꞅɑ, a cloak of silk.
Sıol, *n. m.* seed.
Síoꞃ, *adv.* below.

8

Síop, *adv.* down.
Siotcáin, *n. f.* peace.
Sípe, emph. form of pí.
Siúbail, *v.* walk, travel.
Siúbal, *v.* (inf.) (to) walk, travel (ag—) travelling.
Siúcpa, *n. m.* sugar.
Slact, *n. m.* good appearance.
Slactṁap, *adj.* in good case.
Sláinte, *n. f.* health.
Sláinteaṁail, *adj.* healthy.
Slán, *adj.* safe, healthy.
Slán, *n. m.* safety, plán leat, fare thee-well.
Sliab, *n. m. & f.* a mountain.
Sluaġ, *n. m.* a multitude, a host.
Sneacta, *n. m.* snow; ag pneacta, snowing.
So, *dem. pron.* this.
Sóġ, *n. m.* joy, pleasure.

Sóiḋeunta, *adj.* possible (easy to be done).
Soilléip, *adj.* bright, lucid.
Soin (form of pin), that, this; pao ó poin, long from that, long ago.
Son, *n. m.* sake; aip pon (*cpd. prep.*), for the sake of, (*with gen.*)
Sona, *adj.* fortunate.
Sonap, *n. m.* happiness.
Spapán, *n. m.* a purse.
Spéip, *n. f.* the firmament.
Sppé, *n. f.* a dowry, cattle.
Spáio, *n. f.* a street.
Spól, *n. m.* satin.
Spotáin *gen.* of a streamlet.
Spotán, *n. m.* a streamlet, also ppután.
Sput, *n. m.* a stream.
Stápaio, *n. m.* a historian; also ptápaioe.

Scuaim, *n. f.* prudence, modesty, artifice.
Suaſ, *adv.* up.
Ṡuaſ, *adv.* above.
Súd, *dem. pron.* there, yonder.
Súgaċ, merry.
Súile, *n. f. pl.* eyes.
Tá, *v.* am, art, is, are.
Tábact, *n. f.* substance.
Tabaiṗ, *v. irr.* give.
Taóg, *n. m.* Teig.
Tae, *n. m.* tea.
Táin, *n. f.* a flock, cattle, a raid.
Táinic, *v. irr. past.* came.
Táinte, *pl.* flocks.
Taiṗbeaċ, *adj.* profitable.
Taiṗiſ, *pr. pron.* over him, it.
Talaṁ, *n. f.* (& *m.*) the earth.
Táll, *adv.* over, yonder.
Talṁan, *gen.* of the earth.
Tan, *n. m.* time, an tan, the time.

Tapaid, *adj.* quick; go tapaid, quickly.
Taſ, *prep.* over.
Taſainn, *pr. pron.* over us.
Taſcuiſne, *n. f.* contempt.
Taſm, *pr. pron.* over me.
Taſt, *pr. pron.* over thee; taſt timċioll, round about.
Taſt, *n. m.* thirst,
Té, *n. m.* the individual; an té, he who.
Teaċ, *n. m.* a house.
Teaċt, *n. m.* a coming teaċt ċugam, coming towards me; *v.* (inf.) to come.
Teaṁaiſ, *n. f.* Tara.
Teaṁpaċ, *gen.* of Tara.
Teanga, *n. f.* a tongue.
Teangain, *dat.* (to) a tongue.
Teangan, *gen.* of a tongue.
Teaſ, *n. m.* heat.
Téid, *v. irr.* go.

Ceuv; *n. m. gen. pl.*
(of) cords; ꞅeubꞃó
ceuv, tearing of
harp-strings.

Ci, *n.* a point; ꞅo v-ci,
until; ꞅiꞃ ci, on the
point (of); ꞅiꞃ ci
beic, on the point of
being, about to be.

Ciꞅ, *v. irr.* comes, come;
ciꞅ liom, (it comes
with me), I can.

Ciꞅ, *dat.* a house.

Cimcioll, *n. m.* a circuit, ꞅ v-cimcioll,
about, (*cpd. prep.
with gen.*) 'nꞅ cimcioll, about him;
cꞅꞃc cimcioll, all
round about.

Cinn, *adj.* sick.

Cinneꞅꞃ, *n. m.* sickness.

Cionól, *n. m.* an assemblage.

Ciꞃ, *n. f.* land, a country.

Ciꞃꞅꞃꞅó, *n. m.* patriotism.

Ciꞃꞅꞃꞅóꞅ, *gen.* of patriotism; muincꞃ ꞅn
ciꞃꞅꞃꞅóꞅ, the patriotic party.

Ciꞃ nꞅ n-óꞅ, the land of the youths.

Cóꞅ, *v.* take, lift; cóꞅ, (past) lifted, also built.

Coil, *n. f.* will, lev'
coil, by your leave.

Coiꞃóeꞅlbꞅc, *n. m.*
Tirloch, Turlough.

Comꞅꞃ, *n. m.* Thomas.

Coꞃꞅó, *n. m.* fruit.

Cꞃe, *prep.* through.

Cꞃeꞅꞃ, *ord. num.* third

Cꞃeun, *adj.* valiant.

Cꞃí, *num.* three.

Cꞃom, *adj.* heavy.

Cú, *pr. pron.* } thou.
Cú, (acc.) } thee.

Cuꞅ, *v. irr.* gave (made).

Cuic; *v.* fall, cuic (past) fell.

Cúꞃ, *n. m.* beginning,
ꞅiꞃ v-cúꞃ, at first.

Cuꞅꞅ, *pers. pron. emph.*
thyself.

133

Ua, *n. m.* a descendant, a grandson.
Ua, *prep.* from.
Uaċtap, *n. m.* the top, the surface, cream, the upper.
Uaiḋ, *pr. pron.* from him.
Uaiġneap, *n. m.* solitude.
Uaim, *pr. pron.* from me.
Uain, *gen.* of a lamb, and *pl.* lambs.
Uainn, *pr.pron.* from us.
Uaiṗ, *n. f.* hour, time; uaiṗ, 'nuaiṗ, or an uaiṗ, the time, when; ca h-uaiṗ, what time, when?
Uaine, *adj.* green.
Uait, *pr. pron.* from thee.
Uan, *n. m.* a lamb.
Uaṗ, *prep.* over, above.

Uaṗail, *dat. fem.* noble.
Uaṗal, *adj.* noble.
Uaṗam, *pr. pron.* over me; or mo ċionn, over my head, now in use.
Uḃ, *n. f.* an egg.
Úḋ, *pron.* there, over.
Uiḃe, *pl.* eggs.
Uile, *adj. pron.* all; ɼo h-uile, entirely; uile ɼo léiṗ, altogether.
Uime, *pr. pron.* about him; uime-ɼean, *emph. form*; uime ɼin, therefore.
Uiṗṗi, *pr. pron.* on her.
Uiɼɼe, *n. m.* water.
Um, uim, or iom, *prep.* about.
Úṁal, *adj.* humble.
Umat, *pr. pron.* about thee.
Úṗ, *adj.* fresh, new.

CRIOĊ.

www.ingramcontent.com/pod-product-compliance
Lightning Source LLC
Chambersburg PA
CBHW022131160426
43197CB00009B/1238